ADVENTURES IN POETRY
Poetorials on JAZZ
and Other Acquired Tastes

Advance praise for

ADVENTURES IN POETRY
POETORIALS ON *JAZZ*
AND OTHER ACQUIRED TASTES

PUBLISHER'S INFORMATION

Author contact: halcrook1@gmail.com

Website: www.halcrook.com

ISBN: 978-1-953080-55-4

© 2024 by Hal Crook

Drawing of the Author by Zoe Crook

Select Author Photos by Joyce Crook

Cover design by Hal Crook

EBookBakery

ADVENTURES IN POETRY
Poetorials on JAZZ
and Other Acquired Tastes

HAL CROOK

"Truth lies in the absurd."

—the Unknown Poet

*"There are many different types of music, one of which is jazz;
and many different types of jazz, some of which are safe."*

—the Unknown Jazzbo

for the anteater I turned out not to be

ACKNOWLEDGMENTS

Before I wrote this book, the material in it had never
been seen or read by a single person except for me,
unless that person happened to be checking out my

Facebook posts in 2023 and parts of 2024, in which
case, some of it may have been seen. But I doubt
read. Except by those courageous folks whose kind

comments are smeared all over pages II-III. But even
if it was seen and read, many words have since been
changed. For the better, I'd say. Although how would

you know for sure if you never read it before? Well,
you wouldn't; so you'll just have to trust me, because
each word has been checked with the word before it,

and also the word after it, to make sure it fits in there
logically. Logic is an important ingredient when cooking
up poetic phrases using words, especially if you want

your readers to understand your points, which I do,
and which I learned the hard way, from writing other
books and being criticized for it when it was missing.

Raked over the literary coals is more like it. (See
the back of this book for where you can buy them.)
But I think you'll find my writing is not the same as

other poetic writers', in that it tends to be different.
In some cases, it's much better, in others not nearly
as good. Sometimes you'll be reading along and

expecting something serious to happen, but it turns out
to be funny instead. Or you might expect it to be funny,
and it turns out to be serious. You just never know. But

don't worry, it'll never be *too* serious, or *too* funny. More
like an unexpected turn of events that just isn't that
remarkable. I call it *milking the absurd for all it's worth—*

which, historically speaking, isn't much. But you can't
just go by history; all it ever wants to do is repeat itself,
which is boring. I'll take my chances with the absurd

any day. Plus, there is truth in the absurd, if you know
where to look for it. Which I seem to know, possibly
from being dropped as a infant. Though not often.

Whereas others have called it illogical. Whimsical.
Also lazy. If you continue to read through the book
the way you're supposed to read one—from front to

back—and don't flit around like a butterfly on crack—
you'll see exactly what I mean. Or maybe you've
already gotten the idea. Of course, the main thing is

to feel you've gotten your money's worth from your
reading experience once you're done with it. To me,
that's always a big deal when I finish reading a book.

Especially if I had to buy it.

And so, now that you have me right where I want you,
let me thank the poets Paul Hostovsky, Ron Koertge,
Rod Kessler, Margie Keil Flanders, and I. Michael

"Milton" Grossman, for invaluable inspiration and
camaraderie. And not only that, but if *their* inspiration
and camaraderie is so invaluable, then my wife Joyce's

is truly indispensable, irreplaceable, and immeasurable.
You can add inestimable and incalculable to that list,
too. Priceless as well. In fact, Joyce is the best thing

that ever happened to things like inspiration and
camaraderie and me. And believe you me, that is
no exaggeration. No hyperbole. No overstatement.

No aggrandizement, elaboration, or excessive puffery.
No transparent gesture to try to appease her for putting
up with my lazy yet whimsically illogical love of the absurd.

Thanks, honey.

CONTENTS

FOREWORD XII

ROUND ONE

JAZZ v. POETRY   2

JAZZ v. CLASSICAL   7

JAZZ v. POP v. ROCK   10

JAZZ v. STOP & SHOP   13

JAZZ v. FREE JAZZ   17

JAZZ v. WAR   21

ROUND TWO

JAZZ v. JAZZ CRITICS   24

JAZZ v. MARRIAGE   29

JAZZ v. JAZZ EDUCATION   31

JAZZ v. SEX   37

JAZZ v. The HOLIDAYS   40

JAZZ v. THINKING v. The ZONE   47

HALF TIME

Featuring Special Guests HOP HOSTOVSKY,
GLISSANDO CROOKINI, and ROBERT FROST   55

ROUND THREE

JAZZ v. SPORTS   58

JAZZ v. The BASTARDS   61

JAZZ v. GOD And RELIGION   65

JAZZ v. ROBERT BURNS And SAINT SYLVESTER
And POPE GREGORY XIII And The BOY SCOUTS
And HUBERT REEVES And The GENERAL PUBLIC   75

JAZZ v. ARTIFICIAL INTELLIGENCE   79

JAZZ v. JAZZ FANS   83

ROUND FOUR

JAZZ v. VETERINARY MEDICINE   90

JAZZ v. PARENTHOOD   95

JAZZ v. WANTING IT v. WANTING To WANT IT   100

JAZZ v. BERKLEE v. MOVING ON   109

JAZZ v. SCOTUS   112

JAZZ v. OLD AGE   117

SUDDEN DEATH ROUND

JAZZ v. CONSCIOUSNESS   123

FOREWORD

As ludicrous as this may sound, this book is
a competition between jazz—an art form I have
practiced and played professionally for most of my
life, which many people consider to be an acquired
taste itself—and numerous other subjects that may
have the feel or vibe of an acquired taste to them.

Though for some of these subjects, you will have to
use your imagination a little to grasp the connection
to an acquired taste. Or a lot. Or not at all, if you're
a certain kind of person. Like, *a little bit off* is good.
Or a lot. So relax, because who isn't?

Each piece is written in the style of a narrative
editorial, but expressed in the form of a poem,
e.g., using stanzas and line breaks—like this one—
and other elements of poetry as well, such as clichés
—those old familiar sayings used to help the reader
understand what the writer is talking about.

Know what I'm saying?

I was planning to write each piece as a strict poem,
but after years of trying to write strict poems, I still
haven't figured out exactly what a strict poem is,
or how to write a good one, or even a bad one.
I'm afraid if it's strict poetry your looking for here,
you'll need a lot more imagination.

Maybe more than there is.

So I gave up on that idea and just wrote everything
down as poetically as I could, and then tried to give it
a good solid appearance of poetry. Then I got the idea
to combine the words *poetry* and *editorial* and out
popped the word "poetorial" (po-e-tor-i-al)—which
to me best describes what the writing looks like
on the page and sounds like in my head.

I'm talking the creative part of my head, where my
imagination stays up late, drinks too much, carouses

with undesirables, frightens the dog, and hangs out in its underwear. (Shh. The kids might be watching.)

The book is organized in 4 sections, or "Rounds"—to use a cool boxing metaphor (another element of strict poetry, by the way)—with 6 poetorials in each Round.

I've termed the 4 Rounds a "poethon" (po-e-thon), a cool pun I made up on the word marathon—using even more imagination and making it all feel like an honest-to-goodness tournament.

Each poetorial is a contest between the Home Team (Jazz) and the Visitors (Acquired Tastes), at the end of which a winner is chosen based on specific criteria known only to an imaginary judge, or in some cases a whole panel of imaginary judges.

These folks are so imaginary that even I don't know who they are. Which is probably for the best. But hey, at least I'm not breaking the laws of physics by writing imaginary poetorials with real judges in them!

And as far as the narration goes, you would expect *me* to be narrating each piece in the book, right? Well, don't count on it. To keep things interesting and ensure a consistent level of absurdity throughout, other voices in my head will butt in from time to time and completely take over. And don't even bother asking who these voices belong to. Remember, *this is not strict poetry*.

A running score is kept and included after each poetorial, so you don't have to stay sober enough to remember it, or keep turning the pages back to find out. (Your welcome.)

All you classic poetic types out there will probably think this is jejunely puerile, or drolly risible, or fatuously farcical—especially if you know what those words mean. (I had to look them up, myself.) And I hear you.

But try to be a little patient and understanding, because what I'm doing here has never been done before, and so who knows what's going to happen.

If this stuff catches on with the poetic public,
you might be sorry for pooh-poohing it.

Besides, have you ever done something with your
poetry—or with anything else in life—that no one
has ever done before? Believe me, it's cool.

You don't have to sit and listen to anyone criticize
you or correct you or tell you to do it this way or
that way or *hey you're doing it all wrong.*

I mean, what do they know about it that you don't?
Absolutely nothing. Heck, it's never been done
before. No one's ever even wanted to try!

And remember: I might be a troubled poet—and
more than a little bit off myself—but I'm the one
with a big head start on becoming a successfully
troubled poetorialist, too. You would've had to
start writing hours ago to catch up to me.

Not to be snarky, but keep that in mind before
you start rolling your eyes and scoffing yourself
into a coma over what you're about to read,
and maybe come to appreciate and enjoy.

Like any other acquired taste.

After all, the book is titled *Adventures* In Poetry,
not *Playing It Safe* In Poetry, or *Same Old Same
Old* In Poetry, or *Been There Done That* In Poetry.

And with that...

Man Your Battle Stations In Poetry!
Choose Your Weapon In Poetry!
Take No Prisoners In Poetry!

AND LET THE GAMES BEGIN!

♫ ♫ ♫

The author playing duo with Dad (1950).
Looks like he's either having fun or passing gas.
Probably both. Some things never change.

—ROUND ONE—

HOME TEAM: Jazz 0; VISITORS: Acquired Tastes 0.

JAZZ v. POETRY

My first thought is a question: What if the reader
doesn't care about jazz, or poetry either? Even an
award-winning poetorial about universal stuff like
life and death—which you would think everyone
would care a lot about—would likely lose. To jazz.

In which case, how discouraging for poetorialists.
Who must now get used to the idea that not everyone
cares about the same universal stuff they do, or as
much as they do, and deal with it like discouraged
but responsible practitioners of the art form.

And regarding jazz: Imagine what a jazzman—and
especially a jazz woman—has to do to get listeners
interested in what they play, instead of how they look.

And then what they have to play to keep from getting
booed off the stage for not looking good enough.
And for jazz players, any chance to even get on a
stage—any stage, anywhere—can take a miracle.
Unless they look *really* good.

Which can take yet another miracle.

And then to stand up there making what many
consider to be these pet-shop-on-fire type noises
for a few lonely people from different walks of life—
some of whom are in a bad mood to begin with,
knowing they have to get up early to get the kids
ready for school and then rush off to a job
they hate (your basic universal stuff),

unlike your jazz practitioner, who gets to sleep in
to replenish his or her energy for tomorrow night's
performance, whether there is one or not (your basic
non-universal stuff)—well, it's just a super iffy way to
communicate your deepest emotions and feelings
through your musical instrument.

At least poets get to use words, some of which the
public may know—along with some innocent beret
wearing and finger snapping and bongo drumming—

versus all those endless scales and nerve-wracking arpeggios—to help you understand what they're trying to say.

What can jazz players do? Play louder? Higher? Faster? More off key? Is that even possible?

Also, with poetry you can ask questions, and there will likely be someone more poetic than you standing around who will love to answer them. Like a poet. Or a critic: someone who makes a living explaining

the mysteries of the greatest poets' poetry—and so the more mysterious the better, right? Because critics need jobs, and poets need prizes, and the public needs authority figures. (What a racket.)

Again, using words—which you probably won't know this time. But there are non-mysterious books, called dictionaries. Used by poets and critics alike, just to keep you guessing. (It's all part of the scam.)

But just try asking one simple question about jazz. For instance, "Why do you bother?" The answer will likely come back in the form of—yup, you guessed it—*more jazz.*

With your jazz professionals responding by playing even weirder stuff than the stuff they're being asked about. In fact, statistics show that 1 out of every 3 jazz players *sounds just as weird* as the other 2! Which can cost critics their jobs.

And then where would we be?

So maybe poets shouldn't feel so discouraged after all—like they've made a big mistake by choosing poetry for a profession. Because in reality, you cannot choose poetry for a profession because poetry is not even a profession.

Throughout the ages, major poets have shown time and time again that nobody knows exactly

what poetry is, but almost everyone agrees—
it's definitely not a profession.

A profession is something you can do to make
money. Maybe not a lot, but at least a little.
So forget poetry if it's money you're after.
Jazz too, by the sounds of it.

Not to slip in an old worn out cliché at the end
of an informative poetorial, but it bears repeating
that: YOU don't choose poetry. IT chooses you.

Or else it doesn't, like in my case. And in many
famous poets' cases, too, by the way.
From what I've read anyway.

Either way, be glad it's poetry and not jazz.

HOME TEAM: Jazz 0; VISITORS: Acquired Tastes 1.

♫ ♫ ♫

JAZZ v. CLASSICAL

Music is one of those super subjective subjects
—like poetry or beer or wine or board games—
where either you like a certain kind or you don't.

Some folks like it all—all kinds—which might mean
there's something wrong with them. The people,
not the kinds. Maybe they're needy. Or lonely.

Or bored. And then there are those who'll tell you
outright they have better things to do with their time
than waste it on music and poetry and board games.

Maybe because they've had too much beer or wine.
Or not enough. But if you've had just the right amount,
you'll usually like one kind of a thing better than another.

And the reason pretty much always comes down to
personal taste. Or personal finance. Or personal
snobbery. Take jazz music compared to classical,

since that's the title of this poetorial. Two different
styles, but also similar. People usually prefer one
over the other, though, depending on the situation.

For washing the car, they like jazz. For washing
the windows or the dog, it's classical. But it's all just
music, right? Just a bunch of innocent notes buzzing

around in our ears, keeping us awake or asleep and
in the right mood, right? Wrong! Wasn't it the great
jazzman Duke Ellington who said, "There are two

kinds of music: Good music—*and the other kind.*"?
He could have been talking about Country Western
music, which certain music elitists might say sounds

a lot like *the other kind*. Especially if they live in a
big city back East. Or, he could have meant
something called smooth jazz, otherwise known as

elevator music. Because people have been known
to die violently in elevators, supposedly from the
music. Or from when it makes the cables snap.

(Doesn't bother me. I always take the stairs.)

But it's important to be able to tell the difference
between jazz and classical music, so here are a few
hints about how to keep them separate in your mind.

Both styles use the same tiny black dots for notes,
but classical uses more sharps, jazz more flats.
Enharmonically speaking. Both styles tend to use

too many. And sometimes not enough! They both use
the same fascinating rhythms as well, but classical
rhythms land on the (boring) downbeat, giving you

a headache, while jazz lands on the (nervous) upbeat,
giving you a stomachache—causing many fans to drink
more beer and wine than they should at musical events.

And finally, they both use the same harmonies, some
mundane, others shocking—depending on the date of the
music—with classical grabbing the happy endings, jazz

the sad. And as far as dancing goes, it's generally not
recommended with either style, unless you know how
to jitterbug on top of a piano, or twirl around the room

like an angelic ballerina. Either way, both kinds of music
are considered good and not *the other kind.* Which—in
case you're wondering—saves time and lessons by

using the same notes over and over again; with no
sharps or flats—ever; and only one basic rhythm,
which goes well with the moonshine you guzzle while

do-si-do-ing at gun point; and a single universal
harmony—so they can start the song anywhere and
end it anywhere and everybody's happy because

you can't mess it up. And what's not to like about
that? But now the German judge is insisting that
classical should win the poetorial because all

the biggest names in music play it, and like it.
Like Bach, Beethoven, and Brahms. Even Liberace.
Apparently the German judge is the only one

on the planet who's never heard of the world-
famous jazz trumpet player, Neal Armstrong, who
played his trumpet on the moon! You can't get a

bigger name than that. So I say we compromise
and give each style—jazz and classical—a single
point. What's not to like about that?

HOME TEAM: Jazz 1; VISITORS: Acquired Tastes 2.

JAZZ v. POP v. ROCK

The more you hear about these styles of music
—in particular, the lives they ruin, the damage

they cause to livestock and property, the devastating
effects they have on climate change and so on—

the more the idea of replacing them with new and
more utilitarian styles sounds good. However, by

now they're pretty famous and well-established
and aren't going anywhere fast. Or at any other

speed either. Musically or otherwise. I've checked.
Hoped. Prayed. Threatened. Harassed.

But, looking on the positive side, at least jazz is
not still coming up the river—flooding the banks

along the way, destroying homes and villages,
poisoning fish and wildlife—having finally settled

in places like New Jersey, New York, New London,
New Hampshire, New Brunswick, and Newfoundland.

With its bastard cousins—pop and rock—tagging
along like malignant tumors. Causing serial

inbreeding and producing freakish hybrid
forms, like pop-jazz, and rock-jazz, and snap-

crackle-pop-rock-jazz—with its demonic disciples
living on ayahuasca neat, with ketamine chasers.

Pop music (short for popular, or so spineless even
politicians like it) is known for its debilitating lack of

family values, and having no healthy sense of self
whatsoever. Best played live at smoldering campfires,

and limited in scope to needle drops in made-for-
TV-rom-com-movie soundtracks, or to anything

that goes much better in the distant background
of anything else, including distant backgrounds.

Rock music (short for rock'n roll, or offensively
loud pop music) has no moral compass, the worst

breath of any style, and fancies eating its young.
Best played naked at satanic rituals and MAGA

conventions; limited in scope to train wrecks,
teen love, and war; and which is impossible to

keep securely in the background of anything else
without it (the music) being manacled to the wall.

So go ahead and enjoy these miscarriages of
music if that's how you want to live your life.

Just keep the kids away from the windows. Good
idea to change the locks and passwords regularly.

And let's hope they approve a vaccine soon.
The judges can moan and complain all they

want; these poetorials will need respectable
acquired tastes if they want to see some winners.

HOME TEAM: Jazz 1; VISITORS: Acquired Tastes 2.

🎵🎵🎵

JAZZ v. STOP & SHOP

Meet Billy, my jazz trombone student. He will
be starring in this poetorial, along with me
and a few others.

Billy is a savvy but shy young person.
Notice how rough and stained his hands are
from mowing lawns to pay for his lessons.
Which he says mean the world to him.

Watch as he sits patiently in the waiting area,
reminiscent of a painting by Henri Marie
Raymond de Toulouse-Lautrec (1864–1901).

Billy picks up a jazz CD from the display case
and reads aloud about my background. He does
this before each lesson, with the same CD.

He's not what you would call a very good student.
Or even a fair one. Not even average, really.
But not so bad for a metaphorical one.

Still, I try to teach him what I know. Not all at once,
of course. Because nothing happens all at once.
Especially not with jazz.

Which Billy realizes, and so has decided to
keep up his lawn-care business. A smart move,
I tell him, at his lesson each week.

We are covering the blues today. Your basic
12-bar form. In simple keys. Namely C and F.

Lautrec had a rare condition known as
pycnodysostosis (pycno-dyso-stosis),
which made his legs very short.

In addition to alcoholism, he developed
an affinity for brothels and prostitutes.

♫ ♫ ♫

Billy enters the studio and sits down. "Sorry,
Mr. Crook," he says. "I couldn't practice this
week. I have to cut a lot of lawns to pay for
these trombone lessons."

"What about the week before last, Billy?" I say.
"And the week before that…when it snowed?"

"Also, I plow," Billy says.

The unruly beast of an instrument looks brutishly
trapped in the grip of his metaphorical hands.
Reminiscent of a painting by Henri Marie
Raymond de Toulouse-Lautrec.

Billy opens the spit valve at the bottom of his
trombone slide and blows into the mouthpiece
at the other end. A wad of grub-colored slime
splatters onto the floor of the studio.

"You missed the rag again, son," I say.
Then, "Let's turn to page 4."

Billy finds the rag and opens the spit valve
and blows hard again. Then finds page 4.

"Blue Monk," he says, reading the song's title.
"In the key of…wait…is that B flat?"

"Correct," I say.

"But we've been doing the simple keys.
Namely C and F."

"Yes," I say. "B flat is the next one."

"But yesterday I hurt my elbow digging up a
tree stump," Billy says. "Plus, I have to plow."

While Billy was busy digging a tree stump out of
the frozen ground, I was visiting the post office.
Which isn't hiring. And won't be any time soon.

I'm grateful Stop & Shop still needs baggers.

Along with Cézanne, Gauguin, Seurat,
and van Gogh, Lautrec figures as
an important post-impressionist.

♫ ♫ ♫

At the post office I run into Billy. He stands
behind the counter looking official in his new
postal service uniform. As I approach, he
drops a metaphorical package into the bin.

"I'm sorry you're not teaching jazz trombone
lessons anymore, Mr. Crook," he says.

"Well, Billy," I say. "It was time."

"I hope it wasn't my fault," he says. "You know,
for not practicing." He smiles sheepishly. "Ever."

"No, Billy," I say. "You did the best you could.
What with grass to cut and snow to plow.
Stumps to dig."

The other customers are staring. "Ah-hem,"
one of them says. They want their service.

"We all do the best we can, Billy," I say. "Even if
it doesn't come out that way. Like with your
trombone playing," I say. "My poetry."

"Speaking of poetry," he says, holding up
a metaphorical book. Then another.

I stare at the books. Somehow it all feels vaguely
reminiscent of a painting by Henri Marie
Raymond de Toulouse-Lautrec.

Billy hands them to me. "I found them on Amazon."

I read the title of the first book. "Group Poems,"
I say. Then the second. "Adventures In Poetry."
Then, "Hmm. What's a po-e-tor-i-al?"

Billy points a metaphorical finger. "Says on the cover."

Squinting at him I say, "I know these books."

"You should," Billy says. "You wrote them."

♫ ♫ ♫

Bagging at Stop & Shop has not been going so
great. But the post office isn't hiring. Except for
Billy. Whose customers grow impatient.

In 2005, an early painting by Lautrec of a young
laundress—titled *La Blanchisseuse*—sold for
22.4 million dollars.

The buyer was almost certainly not a postal
worker, or a grocery bagger, or a trombone player.
More likely, the buyer owned STOP & SHOP.

Making me wonder if the buyer would like
to own a trombone. Used.

HOME TEAM: Jazz 1; VISITORS: Acquired Tastes 3.

JAZZ v. FREE JAZZ

"Nothing in the whole wide world of jazz
sounds worse than bad free jazz—except
maybe bad free jazz scatting."

Childish, nervy, delusional—the above quotation
comes from a book called *Beyond Time and Changes:
A Musician's Guide to Free Jazz Improvisation.*

Written by traditional-jazzman-turned-free-jazzman-
turned-novelist-turned-short-story-writer-turned-poet-
turned-poetorialist—Hal Crook—who is still turning
into things and will likely continue to do so unless
someone grabs a hammer quick and...

The point is—or should've been—that there are
many different types of music, one of which is jazz;
and many different types of jazz, some of which are
safe. Like ragtime, Dixieland, swing, bebop, post bop,
neo bop, and neonatal-postpartum-hard-bop.

After these you'll come up against your more risky
and adventurous modern forms, for which you'll need
electricity, indoor plumbing, and a roof—such
as amplified-bop, electronic-bop, digital-bop, and
www.https://great_deals_on_amazon_bop.

From here—if you're not careful—you'll run straight
into your hot-headed, gun-toting, scripture-quoting,
Bible-pounding, ultra-conservative styles, such as
Proud-bop, MAGA-bop, Conspiracy-Theory-bop,
Skin-Head-bop, and Super-Scary-Right-Wing-
Neo-Nazi-Evangelical-Militia-bop.

Balanced (more or less) by your signature-gathering,
voter-registering, rude-hand-gesture-hurling, ultra-
liberal styles, such as ANTIFA-bop, LGBTQ-bop,
Woke-bop, Bop-Lives-Matter, and Me-Too-Bop.

Of all these styles of jazz, free jazz is the most
dangerous and fun to play, due to the whole
no-mistakes thing, as in you cannot make any.

Especially in places like Florida, where you can
load it into your AR-15 and wipe out the competition
in a single chorus at jam sessions and fashionable
all-night book burnings; and in Texas, where they
play it at the border to prevent legal crossings and
separate immigrants from their families, and souls.

Not that free jazz can't get the joint jumping when
played at the highest levels, requiring all players
to improvise simultaneously with no musical
boundaries—meaning no predetermined tempo
or meter or song form to guide their playing—as
they somehow make the music sound like a popular
song they've been practicing and playing for years.

(See for yourself at: https://halcrook.com/videos.)

It happens. It can be done. And Mount Everest can
be climbed, too. But in case it can't, here are some
additional free-jazz fun facts to keep the nightmares
coming:

1. Free jazz has no melodic or rhythmic or harmonic
conscience, and wouldn't be caught dead defending
the rights of minorities, or donating to a worthy cause.

2. Last year's Grammy Award for Best Free Jazz
Performance went to a 9-car pile-up on the New
Jersey turnpike.

3. Those who play free jazz need to think about
what it does to healthy brain tissue in the unborn.

4. People who like free jazz like other free things too,
such as: shampoo samples, parking passes, movie
tickets, construction estimates, and consultations.

5. Free jazz is classified by the Drug Enforcement
Administration as a Schedule 1 Controlled Substance.

6. It is available at CVS and Walgreens, but only with
a prescription signed by Ornette Coleman, Eric Dolphy,
and the current Speaker of the House, Mike Johnson.

7. Blue Cross and Medicare do not cover it, either by its generic name—jazzinflictapane—or brand names such as Aciddajaz, Musick, and Toasted.

8. In liquid form, it will melt steel.

9. They play it under trees and they die. The trees do.

10. Many players of free jazz charge nothing for their services, which is totally worth it.

11. It is a felony to listen to free jazz while operating heavy farm machinery.

12. No one has ever been able to play free jazz and chew gum and climb Mount Everest at the same time.

13. Hence, if regular jazz and free jazz are the only kinds of jazz allowed, regular jazz will win as the general listener's preferred style.

14. Unless the general listener happens to be a general contractor who wants to clear a lot full of trees, or sink a battleship, or turn a cow into a puddle of reddish milk, or take the New Jersey turnpike to work.

HOME TEAM: Jazz 2; VISITORS: Acquired Tastes 3.

♫ ♫ ♫

JAZZ v. WAR

The United Nations recognizes 195 countries in the
world today, of which at least 29 are at war. That's 29

too many, according to anyone not profiteering from it.
Clearly, these countries need more jazz spots. Such as

a jazz club, a jazz school, a jazz society, a jazz band
or two in each city, town, village, mountain or dessert

enclave, etc., to cheer up the fighters and get them
off the battlefield and into the bars. I'll bet even

the enemy would enjoy listening to some music,
chilling to the beat, clapping their hands on 2 and 4

with the locals, auditing jazz classes at the school,
taking up an instrument, sitting in with the band on

open-mic nights, playing their favorite songs, singing
along and even dancing! Otherwise it means more

bloodshed and power outages and food and water
shortages and homelessness and refugee camps

and humanitarian corridors and a lot more of these
foreign photo-journalist teams setting up cameras

all over the place and asking triggering questions
such as why are you guys so mad at each other and

can't we all just grab a beer at this hopping jazz joint
down the street called *Hal's Hideaway* and try to work

things out? There's a hot little band playing there
featuring the sensational Italian jazz trombonista—

Glissando Crookini—who you don't get to hear play
anymore because he quit in 2016 and now spends all

his time writing poetorials, which come out good and
all, but nowhere near good enough to put an end to

war or solve the kinds of problems that cause it to start
in the first place. So the molto-swinging, molto-swaying

Glissando has decided to get out his trombone one last
time and—with virtually no chops left after not playing

for so long—do his best to put everyone in a better
mood. You know, get them all swinging and swaying to

the universal sounds of jazz—or at least to the regional
and local sounds—which might seem like a trivial solution

to some because the answer to serious conflict is never
that easy or simple. But on the other hand, anything

is better than war, even a whole night of jazzy
trombone glissandi. But now that I see the idea

in print, I really think it would be wise for the great
Crookini to read a poetorial or two between numbers

—maybe even this one!—in case the warriors reject
the medium of jazz and prefer the medium of poetry,

or in case the sound of a trombone is just too
irritating to relax to and enjoy the company of hostile

combatants with. It's too bad jazz never even stood a
chance to win this poetorial. How sad is it to lose to

—of all things—war! Let's hope the United Nations
is paying close attention to it all. And not profiteering.

HOME TEAM: Jazz 2; VISITORS: Acquired Tastes 4.

—ROUND TWO—

HOME TEAM: Jazz 2; VISITORS: Acquired Tastes 4.

JAZZ v. JAZZ CRITICS

We all have our own opinions about jazz, right?
Some worth more than others—depending on
who's saying what about whom to whom. Which
is why it's wise to consider the source before
taking anything anyone says too seriously.

Like, it's one thing when your Auntie Connie smiles
lovingly and says *Gee Billy, your jazz playing is
getting jazzier by the minute, love all the high notes*
—and quite another thing when Louis Armstrong
leaps back to life and yells *Yessssss!* after you
blow 8 bars on "Mack the Knife."

Now that's an opinion. But back to your aunt.

What does your Auntie Connie know about jazz
that would qualify her impression of your playing
as something you'd want to take to heart?

Is her last name Ellington? Monk? Coltrane?
Is she on the cover of this month's Jazztimes?
Or Jazziz? Or Jazz Player? Jazz Aunties, at least?

Has she spent hours every day of her life practicing
inside a tiny windowless cubicle? Played multiple
jam sessions each week with no-swinging rhythm
sections? Soloed night after night on dark
street corners in bad neighborhoods for years,
till the big break finally comes and she moves
out of the elements and down into the subway?

And what if you happen to play the piccolo and she
can't tell one high note from the next? (Who even can,
on a piccolo?) And even if she *has* made it to the
subway, it's a long way from there to playing free
concerts at the Y.

Then the last thing you'd expect to hear is that dear
old Auntie Connie has been offered a job with a major
music magazine, writing reviews of performances by
living, breathing, and of course complaining, jazz
artists—giving fiction a real run for it's money.

But if in fact she *has* done the work, and does take
the job, and her last name is Gillespie, or Rollins,
or Blakey, at least you'd know she's been living her art.
And so her critique of your playing will be somewhat
informed, and maybe worth consideration.

Not just by you, by the way, but by all her readers.
Your audience. Fans. Peers. Even your heroes.

Now don't get all nervous and depressed over it.
She's probably not going to trash you, she's your
aunt for god's sake. Unless it becomes painfully
clear that you have not done the work, in which
case, let's face it, you deserve to be trashed.

However, if she's a player herself she'll know
firsthand what you're up against, and what you must
succeed at in order to get in the game and stay there.
So she'll probably be compassionate and emphasize
the positive aspects of your playing in her reviews.
Provided there are any.

But don't expect her to jeopardize her own jazz rep
and say you sound great if you don't. And would you
even want her to? (Say no. At least look contrite!)

You have to *earn* compliments like that from respectable,
jazz-playing jazz critics. Prove your ability beyond any
doubt to the whole world, not just to a blood relative
who got a little tipsy one night and agreed to help
out her kid brother's kid—you, in this case,
a piccolo-playing wannabe jazzbo.

Now imagine what the opinion of a critic who has
not done the work would be worth—to you and to
the world; how uninformed that review would be;
how useless any negative criticism would be, coming
from such a limited source; yet how damaging to your
career! Never mind the vibe at family gatherings.

Negative criticism from someone who never takes
part in the battle, never comes face-to-face with the
enemy, just hides out behind a name until the fighting

is over, then suddenly appears out of nowhere and
stabs the wounded. You, again, in this case.

And not just once, say, in the butt. But in print.
So over and over and over again. In the heart!

Believe it or not, there is work for these creatures
in the critic business.

So Billy, here's another opinion. Not saying whose
it is, but for whatever it's worth, if I were you,
I'd be darn proud of your Auntie Connie.

I'd be thanking her up and down for having the
integrity and the professionalism and the basic
human decency not to print negative criticism,
unless she can do as well or better herself.

She's a credit to your family's name—whatever
it is—and a noble example to critics everywhere.

I'd just try to be more like her. In fact, I'd get up
off that couch right now and turn off the TV and
pull the shades and start working on my *low* notes.

That's right, Billy. You heard me. Before I tell you
whose opinion this really is and she calls her
brother and they make you change your name.

HOME TEAM: Jazz 3; VISITORS: Acquired Tastes 4.

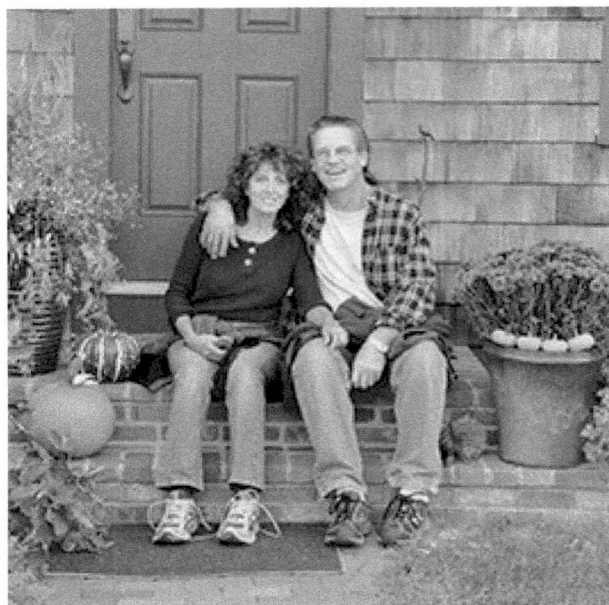

♫ ♫ ♫

JAZZ v. MARRIAGE

As far as any dedicated jazz player might be thinking
after reading the title of this poetorial, the "v." for
"versus" may seem misleading, because jazz is
an art form that requires the musician and the music
to be in a kind of marriage situation all its own;

meaning that if you want to be any good at it (jazz,
I'm talking) you have to spend hours and hours
every day alone in a comfortable air conditioned
practice studio, and do so for years and years—
sort of like an eternal musical honeymoon—where

you receive your meals and messages and bebop
cigarettes through a slot in the door, as if you had
leprosy, while playing your jazz melodies and rhythms
and harmonies and your jazz modes and scales
and recordings to your heart's content;

and by your heart's content I mean you have to
really like it—no, sorry, you have to *love* it—so that
you'll want to stay in there by yourself, just you and
jazz, for at least the minimum 10,000 hours it takes
to become disappointingly adequate;

but that's not all, because then you have to spend
additional hours each day playing all-night jam
sessions in the same old ripe practice room—getting
to know the sweaty new players who'll be replacing
the old ones after they die tragically from leprosy—

in order to be prepared in case your band has to
leave the practice room at some point in your
professional career and play high-profile concerts,
gigs, tours, and recording sessions, which means
you can't be stopping every two months to bathe

or brush your teeth or comb your hair or worry
about how to feed the family or pay the mortgage
or open the fridge; and oh my god after you throw
in a few kids and pets and in-laws and a car loan
it's gonna make the usual kind of marriage—you

know, the typical loving/caring kind (which takes
more loving and caring than you could ever imagine)
—much harder (and shorter) than it should be;
and so by now you can definitely see how the title
of a poetorial like this could absolutely use the word

"versus" between the words "Jazz" and "Marriage"
if the marriage you envision involves jazz and
yourself and another human person, in which case
the "v." would be totally accurate and correct
and not the least bit misleading;

except, of course, if the other person happens
to be a jazz player also, in which case the "v."
would require one of you to musically accompany
the other one, and do so forever, or for as long
as you want to stay married, which,

when you check the statistics, probably isn't such
a good idea (to marry a jazz player, I mean), unless
it's already too late; implying that jazz and marriage
should never have been combined in a poetorial
in the first place, not even with a "v." between them,

because jazz will dominate the situation mercilessly,
won't even try to hide its demanding nature, its
uncompromising self-centeredness, its predilection
for bullying, while marriage just sits there and takes it,
proving that marriage may indeed be an institution,

but jazz is institutionalization.

HOME TEAM: Jazz 4; VISITORS: Acquired Tastes 4.

JAZZ v. JAZZ EDUCATION

But can you even have jazz—or anything else
for that matter—without automatically being
educated by it while you're having it?
Doesn't everything involve education
once the Genie's out of the bottle?

You get your first taste of jazz and your jazz
education begins. You ask the Genie what
instrument you should play and your education
continues. You ignore the Genie's advice and
choose the trombone—because you like a nice
parade or a circus. More education.

A big mistake too, but all part of the learning process.

You take lessons. Education. Learn how to read
music. Education. You practice hard and work on
your pedal tones and glissandos. Education.

You memorize tunes and play jam sessions and
take improvised solos on trombone. When they
let you. You form a band, buy a tux, borrow some
mutes. Do gigs, lose gigs, stand for hours in the
unemployment line wishing you listened to the
Genie and chose the guitar. Or the drums.

The musical saw, the jug, the conch, anything!
You wonder if there's still time. Each experience
an important part of your jazz education.

You meet academic types who wear suits and carry
briefcases and take the whole jazz education thing
so seriously they decide to build schools. You enroll
in an educational jazz program, hoping your jazz
education will become more...well...educational.

The schools hire the jazz players to teach the jazz
students. Another mistake—but who knew teaching
it would be so much harder than playing it?

Impossible, even.

You think about the old maxim: Those who can, do;
those who think others can also, teach; those who
can't do or teach, teach jazz.

The jazz players audition the jazz students and then
rate them. Everyone gets upset. Then depressed.
Then high.

Someone counts off an uptempo tune in the key of
B—which you play in C because you play better
in C—and your formal jazz education begins.

The musical language of jazz gets codified to
everyone's delight. Except for foreign students
who don't speak English, but have wealthy parents
who can pay full price no problem.

New rules and regulations are passed that outlaw
certain notes—like B# and Cb—along with any
chord with an accidental in the chord symbol.

Other notes—like F—are forbidden to be played
or written or even spoken of on major chords,
unless resolved immediately to E.

Tension natural 13 on minor 7th chords gets the
boot, too. All altered tensions are demonized. Vilified.
Condemned. Something about sounding suspicious.
Untrustworthy. Or just plain criminal.

All of which gives you something to discuss in class,
and write in your notebook, and take a surprise quiz
on later, and get charged good money for now!

In return for jazz degrees, diplomas, and textbooks.
T-shirts, ashtrays, and collectable jazz action figures.

The classrooms fill up and the schools start making
money, but everyone wants some so there's never
enough to go around. Only to renovate the
Presidential bathroom.

The administrators want to control the teachers—
who unionize to protect their jobs. The teachers want
to control the students—whose parents unionize to
protect their grades. The students and parents want
to control the administrators—who just ignore them.

The jazz players just want to play jazz and
get high and stay there.

Jazz wants to get the Genie back in the bottle.

Soon, jazz education becomes a power grab.
A business. No, a corporate enterprise. Actually,
a global industry! Complete with sweat-shops,
lawyers, lobbyists, college and high school festivals,
and—everyone's favorite—*competitions.*

Offering cash prizes and grants and scholarships
—*the Darwin Awards*—for the winners; t-shirts and
action figures for the losers; tuition increases for
foreign students whose parents pony up no problem.

Institutionalization sets in. International jazz educator
associations crop up. With jazzy acronyms and logos
and slogans and shiny brochures. And officers and
sponsors and supreme court justices in their back
pocket, with off-shore bank accounts, a navy,
and hefty membership dues…to fund the militias!

Conferences are held in tropical climates where
hordes of jazz educators from all over the planet
gather to network and advance their jazz knowledge,
as they drink colorful cocktails and have colorful
debates on how to improve or at least manipulate
jazz education to everyone's musical and financial
benefit.

"More ascending chromatic II V's in odd meters with
swing feel," touts one educator from the West.

"Modal progressions at dirge-like tempos with straight
8ths," counters a second from the East.

"Mandatory voice leading by half step at the point of chord change," insists a third from the North.

"Uniforms and guns and scantily clad God-fearing vocalists!" demands a fourth from the South."

"A $100.00 fine for anyone calling anyone a 'cat' or a 'chick,' chimes in Human Resources.

All this looks like progress, until someone famous playing in one of the iconic jazz bands hired to entertain the educators looks out on a packed auditorium during his performance and shakes his head—as he leans into the mic and says:

"So much jazz education, so little jazz."

The educators are aghast.

"Could it be true?" moans the president, while quickly scheduling a debate.

Jazz and the Genie, lounging at the bar, sigh in unison. They roll their sad eyes, cover their sore ears, and chug their colorful cocktails.

Then slip out the back, as the debate begins.

HOME TEAM: Jazz 5; VISITORS: Acquired Tastes 4.

♫♫♫

JAZZ v. SEX

Nice to finally have your undivided attention.
Now to hold onto it. Because no one ever picks
me to win. Not even to tie. Not even to survive.

Can't say I blame them. Because in this poetorial,
there's just me—Jazz—an under-appreciated,
hard-to-swallow, acquired taste in music—up against
You-Know-What—a 100% natural and instinctual
feel-good physical act, necessary to relieve tension
and stress and maintain life on the planet, whether
you're a human being, an animal, a plant, or the
current Speaker of the House, Mike Johnson.

Not to mention the most fun you can have
when your parents aren't looking.

Give me a break. How is this a fair match?

I know I can be tiring. Annoying even. Until you
get to know me better. At which point I can be
pretty arousing, too. Maybe not competitively,
as compared to You-Know-What. Although,
in our last match, I had You-Know-What on the
ropes for a few arousing seconds. The judges
said I gave it a good run for its money in some
minor categories—like imagination, practice habits,
and recovery rate. Snazzy outfits was another.

Some say I deserve credit just for getting in the ring
with it. Because it takes guts—in the form of balls—
to go head to head with something that doesn't even
have a head. Does amazing things with its other body
parts, though. To win votes. As if it needed them.

And how do you compete with that? A good beat?
A hot lick? Tickets to the Newport Jazz Festival?

Gimme. A huge. Break.

But I don't feel so bad about losing to it anymore.
Not when I think of all the prominent contenders
that lose to it regularly as well. Like Beauty.

37

And Money. And Love. Even Real Estate.

Even Power—which has the best odds of all—gets
its butt kicked every time. While You-Know-What
has You-Know-What with it in the corner.

Talk about a spectacle. That one'll keep your eyes
open in a sandstorm.

I wonder about the questions they put on the ballot,
too, which seem loaded to me. Questions like:
What gets you more excited below the waist,
naked porn stars having You-Know-What, or
jazz players posing in snazzy vests and ties?

Who would you rather hang out with if
your parents and the Speaker of the House
weren't looking, naked porn stars or
jazz players in snazzy vests and ties?

What demographic group is You-Know-What-y
enough to wear snazzy vests and ties and
make you forget all about your parents and
jazz and the Speaker of the House?

Duh. Hello? Ref? Another break, please.
Make it a double.

Of course, it might help if jazz players were
the only ones allowed to vote. Some of the
sleepier, senile ones might vote for me.
Given the right spread.

Lately there's been talk of letting the underdogs
team up and go after You-Know-What together.
You know, level the playing field. Give us a fighting
chance. Lose—as usual—but at least make
You-Know-What break a sweat now and then.

I'm talking handpicked handicapped teams, like:
Jazz and Poetry v. You-Know-What.
Jazz and Ballroom Dancing v. You-Know-What.
Jazz and Synchronized Swimming v. You-Know-What.
Jazz and Religion and Sports v. You-Know-What.

Jazz and Religion and Sports and Taylor Swift and
the Speaker of the House v. You-Know-What.

We'd still take a terrible shellacking, of course.
But think of all the great You-Know-What
we'd have in the corner while taking it.

And don't forget that there wouldn't even be any
hard-to-swallow jazz to under-appreciate or acquire
a taste for—or any poetry or any ballroom dancing
or any synchronized swimming or any religion or
sports or Taylor Swift or Speaker of the House—
without You-Know-What.

Let's face it: You-Know-What makes the world
go round. Always has, always will. Existence
owes its very existence to it. So maybe it
deserves to win every time.

I mean, can you imagine a world with no poetry?
No ballroom dancing? No synchronized swimming?
No Taylor Swift? No Speaker of the House?

I suppose we could file a complaint with the Bored
of Acquired Tastes for accepting You-Know-What as an
acquired taste in the first place. Because really…what
taste needs to be acquired—by anyone or anything—to
enjoy a little You-Know-What—or even a lot—with
anyone or anything?

HOME TEAM: Jazz 5; VISITORS: Acquired Tastes 5.

JAZZ v. The HOLIDAYS

Who doesn't like a nice holiday? Or better, several.
One right after the other. I'm talking the kind where
you get to stay home from work and celebrate
all day and night with family and friends.

Or even just with friends, if the family's, say, dead.
Or incarcerated. Or out of town. Or if you're not on
speaking terms. And—if you have no friends—just
you and the dog is fine also. Unless you don't have
a dog either, then you and the neighbor's dog.
Perfectly fine. Or just you and the TV is good, too.
I bet you have one of those! Trust me, it'll all work
out. One way or another. Just forget I mentioned it.

Maybe you'll open some carbonated apple juice to go
with a steaming hot dish of Swanson's Microwaveable
Holiday Mac 'N Cheese. And sit by the fire, or the TV
if you don't have a fire, with an attitude—which you
probably will have after a tension-filled holiday
snowball fight with the kids. Oh right, sorry.
With the neighbor's kids, then.

It's especially fun when the holiday falls on a
Friday or a Monday, so you get a nice 3-day
weekend out of the deal. Longer if you're
out of work. Or been laid off. Or fired.

It all sounds great to me. Of course, I'm one of
the lucky ones who still has a family. And a dog.
And a TV. And we're all on speaking terms, too.
Although, I did recently become a poetorialist,
and now there's that pesky downside of not
having a job to take a holiday from.

Still, here's a list of holidays to get us back in the
mood for some nice old-fashioned holiday cheer.
Something to help us forget all about your problems
—if that's even remotely possible at this point.

Let's begin with some familiar government holidays,
like: Presidents Day, Veterans Day, Memorial Day,
Labor Day, Patriot's Day, Election Day (provided you

live in a blue state), and Independence Day—
also known as: July 4th, 5th, 6th, 7th, and 8th—
depending on your tolerance for the hard stuff.

Next come the environmentally conscious holidays,
like: Earth Day, Arbor Day, Endangered Species Day,
National Public Lands Day, World Oceans Day, and
the universally condemned World Plastic Products
Day. Although, I dare anyone to try to get through a
single holiday—or any day—without a plastic fork.

And let's not forget all those highly lucrative holidays
that require love, and, in many cases, forgiveness.
Like: Mother's Day, Father's Day, Children's Day,
Parent's Day, Mother-in-Law's Day, Valentine's Day,
and National Mistress (or Gigolo) Day.

Then there are the inspirational holidays, which we
depend on for…well…inspiration, like: Dignity and
Freedom Day, World Peace Day, Martin Luther King
Jr. Day, Indigenous Peoples Day, Teacher's Day,
and Tax Freedom Day—the kind of holidays we
could use a lot more of, in case you have
a knack for doing heroic deeds.

And we can't leave out the many religious holidays
(as much as we might want to), each one demanding
an unnatural degree of tolerance for other lifestyles,
like: Christmas Day, St. Patrick's Day, All Saints Day
(excluding St. Patrick, since he's already got a whole
day for himself), and countless other holidays that
require membership in a tax-exempt religion, or a
tax-deferred spiritual movement, or a tax-supported
government sponsored cult—like Congress.

And of course there are the musical holidays
which we all like to celebrate, no matter what
beliefs or disbeliefs we can or cannot tolerate, like:
Save the 9-Bar Blues Day, Mixolydian Monday,
Phrygian Friday, and my personal favorite—
Endangered Low Brass Instrumentalists Day.

Also, there are plenty of legitimate holidays that
don't get the attention and respect they deserve, like:

Naked Day, National Gorilla Suit Day, No Pants Day,
International Talk Like a Pirate Day, and National
Sleepyhead Day.

Yup, all 100% for-real holidays. Look them up!

And finally, the eating-and-drinking-yourself-into-
oblivion holidays, like: Thanksgiving Day, New
Year's Eve Day Night, and Super Bowl Sunday.
Technically, every holiday falls into this category,
because what else are you gonna do with family
and friends on holidays—talk politics? Read poetry?

Obviously this list is not as exhaustive as it is
exhausting. And there are a lot more holidays
where these came from. And even more
where they didn't come from!

I'm talking far away places like: the Arctic Circle,
the Bermuda Triangle, Piccadilly Square, and Florida.
Featuring holidays with names like: Flatbed Truck Day,
Assault Weapons Day, and Children's Book Burning Day.

I think you're getting the idea: Life has way too many
holidays for a single style of music—such as jazz—
to compete with in a single poetorial—such as this.

And here's the other thing: The problem with
enjoying the holidays with a guilt-free conscience
is that we start celebrating them when we're kids,
before we even have a conscience, and before
we know anything about all the folks who might
be standing around during a certain holiday with
hurt feelings about it. Maybe even protesting it.

Meaning that there are holidays out there that
make some people feel sad, or frustrated,
or resentful, or angry, or suicidal, or all of the
above, because of the events associated with it.

Like, if certain groups of people plundered or
pilfered or enslaved or otherwise harmed other
groups of people. You know, assholes.

Talk about a holiday-mood breaker.

I mean, sure, jazz has its dark side—its sordid
past, wishful present, and doubtful future.
Everything from too many notes to not enough,
too many chord changes to not enough, too
many long boring drum solos to not enough…
Well, no, yeah, we've had enough of those for sure.

But here again, you get the idea: jazz may hurt
your ears and try your patience and put you in a
non-celebratory holiday mood, but none of that
has ever destroyed your property or your ancestors
or started a war or a genocide just because you
happen to be different from somebody else.

In fact, jazz embraces all kinds of differences.
Look at how well it treats the Bossa Nova.
Upright bass solos. Vocalists!

Granted, there are plenty of holidays you can say
that about, too. World Migratory Bird Day, for one.
But let's be honest, there are also holidays out there
for which you cannot say that, like: January 6th Day,
Juneteenth, National Election Deniers' Day, and
Peaceful Transfer of Power Over My Dead Body Day.

So, as far as this poetorial goes, I think we have to
eliminate all the decent holidays that never did a
single indecent thing to anyone, and then—in all
fairness to jazz—limit the list of competitive holidays
to just the ones that some folks have a problem with.

Like, Self-Appointed Spiritual Leaders Day.
And Let's Give Congress a Raise Day.
And Forfeit Your Seat For A Bully Day.

Now who do you like to win? Or at least to tie?

I say we give Jazz and the Holidays a point each,
so that everyone has something to celebrate!

And by the way, if you're gonna be alone this coming Groundhog Day, I've got a nice bottle of carbonated apple juice I've been saving for a special occasion.

We can warm up the Mac 'N Cheese. Talk politics. Read some poetry. Celebrate Jazz's comeback from the shellacking it took from You-Know-What in the previous poetorial…

You can even bring the neighbor's dog.

Salud!

HOME TEAM: Jazz 6; VISITORS: Acquired Tastes 6.

♫ ♫ ♫

JAZZ v. THINKING v. The ZONE

When eating ice cream, do you greedily indulge in
the thrill of it like a spoiled child on its 2nd birthday,
or do you studiously critique the flavor, viscosity,
frigidity, and sweetness coating your tongue?

On blizzardy nights, do you gleefully relish
the warmth of a raging fire, or do you hunt for a
thermometer to measure the precise temperature
inside the room and log it into your weather diary?

When you get all hot and bothered on a date,
do you kiss your lover sloppily with passion and
abandon, or do you soberly assess the degree of
titillation while considering going to second base?

While improvising a jazz solo, do you hear and feel
the music in every fiber of your being, or do you
judge each note, rhythm, and player while wishing
you majored in finance instead of hospitality?

Perhaps you do all of the above. Or some. Or none.
In any case, the function of thought is to divide the
world into this and that, to separate each experience
into self (subject) and other (object) in order to
better control the outcome. Meaning—to score.

For without the ability to think, and do so wisely,
you won't last an hour out there. Maybe not even
a minute. Not even one quick smooch.
(Trust me, I've tried.)

However, as normal and natural and necessary
as thinking is, in some situations it can impact the
outcome negatively, or undesirably. And not just
because our thinking may be flawed.

But because analyzing and evaluating a situation
typically leads to judgment, which—whether favorable
or unfavorable—prevents us from being one with
the experience by creating the impression that
there is a thinker *separate* from the experience.

An "I" that is causing all the excitement, getting
all the action, having all the fun.

But is there? Does this "I" actually exist as a
separate entity? Can we see it, touch it, smell it,
fondle it, locate it anywhere? Is there a taster
separate from the taste, a kisser from the kiss,
a jazz player from the jazz playing?

Or is there just another thought that keeps
popping up on the heels of all the others?
One that seems to be the brains of the outfit.
The head honcho that's always trying to convince
us that this "I"—this sense of self—is real, and
that it exists corporeally, like, say, a trombone does.

Naturally, it comes as a shock to our ego that this
"I" doesn't exist, especially since our ego does!
(And we all have the scars to prove it, right?)

But things could be worse. Suppose you were a
major voice of the art form—a Coltrane, or a Bird,
or a Monk—and not able to take credit for your
achievements because…well…*you don't exist.*
Those are the folks who have it toughest.

On the other hand, selflessness also means
there's no one there to take the blame for our
lack of achievements, either. So there's a bright
side to it all, too.

What happens, then, when there's no analyzing
or judging going on while we eat our ice cream or
kiss our lover or play our jazz? The mind is still
conscious, but silent. Thought-less. Thinker-less.
Locked in the zone. One with experience—is it not?

More importantly, how do we get our mind into
that blessed state of stillness, of passive alertness,
observant—yet no longer distracted or deluded
by thought?

How do we quell the interruptions of thought—
the main one being the thought of "I", the illusory

self—if in fact there is no self to be found
except in our mind?

And—to really blow our mind—how can thoughts
disrupt our oneness with experience *if there is no
actual self there to be separated from experience
in the first place?*

Hey, don't look at me. I'm just the poetorialist here,
prattling on about this and that. When they said poetry
can be hard to understand, they weren't kidding.

And by the way, if the self isn't real, who are
they talking about when they say "they," as in:
"they say poetry can be hard to understand"?
Who is this "they" anyway? And who do
"they" "think" "they" are?

Not to be a poetic pest, but there is yet another
dimension to all this. Because the taste of ice cream
does not exist on our tongue, nor the sensation of
a kiss on our lips, nor the sounds of jazz in our ears—
but as neuron activity happening inside our brain,
and, therefore, we are as much one with these things
as we are with our blood and bones and all the
other boring stuff going on inside our body.

Neurologically speaking, we *already are* one with
our jazz playing, but—unfortunately—we're just
too self-obsessed to realize it. If we could just get
over ourself a little—meaning our self that doesn't
exist—we might be able to see it. For ourself.

Also, there is the unfortunate fact that the more
we know about a subject the more there is to
not think about when we do think about it.

And so all the super smart jazz Ph.D.'s out there
—trying to get in the zone and play their asses off
without thinking and judging themselves to death—
really have their work cut out for them.

Especially if they still think they exist. But also
because of how sadly they must play now after

spending all that time in school, studying—instead
of in the woodshed, practicing.

See that? Should've taken more playing classes.
Less theory. Too late now. *Ye know too much.*

Because here's what else they say: *Blessed are
the ear players, who know not what they play,
for they shall inherit the bandstand.*

But allow me to assist, since I'm a longtime fan
of illusions. You may be able to achieve the state
of mind you seek, but first you'll have to trash
all your degrees and academic credentials,
which are worthless on the bandstand anyway.

And second, you'll have to practice the following
simple yet impossible exercises, because like
they also say: *As you practice, so do you play.*

Exercise #1: Getting In The Zone. Improvise on
a familiar tune progression, or on a single chord
(modal style), using play-along accompaniment,
where the only goal is to dismiss all thoughts about
your playing (or anyone else's) as they arise while
you play. Whether joyful, regretful, or just plain hateful.

The only thought allowed is the one that acknowledges
when you are thinking about and judging your playing
(or anyone else's). Then you must let even that one go
and continue playing, while you fake the not-thinking-
about-it thing as best you can.

See? Simple. But impossible.

Exercise #2: Staying In The Zone. If you must think,
let your ears do it. That's right, think with your ears—
because this is music, which means sound, which
means you need your ears, which have way bigger
and better brains than you do, anyway.

But do not identify or evaluate what your ears are
hearing, even if it's the piano player cussing out the
bass player for hiring a drummer who drags the tempo

as much as he rushes it. As far as you and your ears go, just be grateful the rhythm section showed up, and never finished high school, or wasted good money on a Ph.D.

Considering how much time you likely spend thinking about your improvising while you play, the habit will no doubt be hard to break. But like everything else, with daily practice you will at least be able to improve your chances of failing less profoundly.

Exercise #3: Failing In The Zone. If indeed you fail profoundly, try practicing Exercises 1 and 2 with your eyes closed. Or better, blindfolded. And no peeking!

Because when your brain is not receiving information from your eyes, it will pay better attention to the information coming from your ears. I mean, what choice does it have? You can't touch jazz.
You can't taste it. And you can't smell it.
Unless it's Ph.D. level bad.

But first your brain will have to freak out. Because brains are super into visuals. They're used to depending on your eyes for everything. Total suckers for the sight of, say, a naked supermodel, a transposed lead sheet, the chord changes of the song scribbled on the back of your diploma.

And still, you cannot think about what your ears are hearing. So here's another tip that may help:

Record yourself practicing these exercises so you can remind your non-existent self that you don't have to think about your improvising while you are playing, because you're going to do it later. When you're sure no one else's non-existent self is listening to it and thinking about it also. Using the recording.

This is a convenient way to release yourself from the responsibility of having to pay attention to your playing while it is bombing so badly.
Not to mention a big relief to your ego.

For additional insight, you can compare this
recording to recordings of your playing when
thoughts and judgments and supermodels
are allowed to interfere as usual.

Don't be surprised, though, if at first there is no
noticeable difference between these recordings.
Especially if you're a lick player—which is another
issue you will want to address after you grow
more…well…talented. Creative. Honest.

Then, someday, it will be time to bring your hard-
earned skill onto the bandstand. And just imagine
the oneness you will feel when the whole band—
even the drummer—is in the zone at the same time.

And not just when getting high on breaks, but when
actually playing together. After getting high on breaks.

One more helpful hint: Fortunately for everyone,
the zone is the zone. And so, recalling the intense
oneness you feel when kissing your lover can be
instructive for helping you get in the zone when
improvising.

Of course, second base would be even better.
If you can manage it. Because—like the Buddhist
judge keeps telling us—*it's all the same stuff.*

Though the Buddhist judge admits he's never
even made it to second base. So there's that.

HOME TEAM: Jazz 6; VISITORS: Acquired Tastes 7.

♫ ♫ ♫

HALF TIME!

We regret to announce that our scheduled Half-Time show featuring the celebrated poet Hop Hostovsky reciting Robert Frost's poem "Stopping by Woods on a Snowy Evening" while the forgotten-but-not-yet-forgiven Italian trombonista Glissando

Crookini serenades the crowd with soothing trombone glissandi —has been cancelled due to the weather. Blizzard conditions, in July. Meaning we must have veered off course and landed somewhere in the woods of—yup, you guessed it—southwest

Argentina. And what a coincidence that it was somewhere in the woods of southwest Vermont where Frost conceived his iconic "snow" poem, then 30 years later attended the World Congress of Writers in Sao Paulo, Brazil, which is reportedly

the closest he got to Argentina. But legend has it he snuck off between readings and visited, making it clear why the whole Half Time show suddenly manifested way the heck down here: *it's the barbecue!* Still, this might be a good time to stretch your

legs. Maybe check out Patagonia while we're here. I know, it's not Hostovsky reading Frost with trombone accompaniment, but when was it ever? (At least visit the bathroom.) And what's wrong with stunning vistas at every turn, paths untrodden by

the masses, virgin forests, vast moving glaciers, your own tube of puma repellent? Just be sure to bring the book with you so you don't miss anything in case Round 3 begins before you get back to your seat. You know how that goes. One more

thing: With or without the combined talents of Hostovsky, Frost, Crookini, and tangy Patagonian barbecue, part 2 of the book will begin shortly, and there are still plenty of spectacular acquired tastes to acquire a taste for, like: Sports, God, A.I.,

the Supreme Court, more hot Jazz. Trust me, these poetorials will be even more informative and whimsical than those you loved in part 1. How nice to know your money was well spent. By the way, this will be the only announcement. Thank you.

—ROUND THREE—

HOME TEAM: Jazz 6; VISITORS: Acquired Tastes 7.

JAZZ v. SPORTS

With jazz you learn how to play your instrument in
the safety and privacy of your home, while enjoying
the guidance of a caring teacher; then you memorize
a few songs that you play at jam sessions with your
friends, and work your way up to live performances,
attended by grateful and cheering audiences, full
of supportive and adoring parents. Yours, mostly.

With sports you build up your body in front of muscle-
bound beasts at the gym, as instructed by a psychotic
trainer; then fight your way onto a team, increase the
death benefit on your insurance, inject performance
enhancing drugs and play scrimmages against rivals,
then work your way up to deadly matches, attended
by drunken fans demanding blood. Yours, mostly.

With jazz the mere mention of competition is an
outrage, a disgrace, a disturbance in the Force; you
play to lose yourself in the music, to transcend your
ego and become one with the band, the crowd, the
cosmos; no scores are kept, no ratings, everyone's a
winner, even the losers, none of which officially exist.

With sports the spirit of competition is a virtue, a
necessary evil, a vital killer instinct; you play to win, to
beat—even beat up!—the other guy; official scores are
kept forever by which your weaknesses are continually
exposed and analyzed on the nightly News, resulting
in ratings, winners and losers, heroes and scum.

With jazz you end up playing on a cruise ship, or for
the circus, or in nursing homes on rainy afternoons;
or, if you have to, you teach marching band and
chorus and CPR in a college, or high school, or
middle school, or homeless shelter, or orphanage.

With sports you end up joining a street gang or
the local militia or S.W.A.T. team; or, if you have
to, you coach kick boxing and cage fighting in
a college, or high school, or middle school, or
rehab center, or state penitentiary.

With jazz your life is a musical quest for peace
and love; it's not important how well you play,
what matters is how much pleasure and joy
your playing brings others.

With sports life is a brutal substitute for war;
it's not important how well you play either,
but how much damage in terms of pain
and suffering your playing causes others.

Maybe this is why I played jazz and not sports.
But loved to watch them. Eat and drink to them.
Get high from them. The victories. The defeats.
The blood. Other people's entirely.

Sure, my jazz playing could've been better, too.
But it beat my panicky negative-yard kick-off returns.
My indecisive body checks. My apologetic left hooks.
My squeamish arguments—more like discussions,
or requests, really—with the referees.

Maybe I should have used some of that competitive
spirit from the 4th stanza to hog the mic more often.
Play longer solos. Win a few Grammys. Get better
promo, better gigs, better money. Draw blood!

Hey guys, transcend this!

The Freudian judge says it's a clear cut case of
latent sexual insecurity, immaturity, and hostility.

Know what I say? Screw the Freudian judge.
Sports wins.

HOME TEAM: Jazz 6; VISITORS: Acquired Tastes 8.

♫ ♫ ♫

JAZZ v. The BASTARDS

Seems no matter how good you get at playing jazz,
someone always comes along and plays it better.
Better at this, or better at that. Or better at everything.

And oh my god, sometimes they bring along a friend
who plays even better than they do. The bastards.

We've all heard stories about these wunderkinds,
and what lousy, upbeat roommates they make.
The musically privileged. The unfairly gifted. The
inexcusably advantaged. The unethically talented.
The obscenely under-aged.

Where are the parents? Aren't they paying attention?
Why are they not controlling their children better?

Kissed by brilliance. Suckled by genius.
Propositioned by opportunity. Destined for fame
and fortune. Born to make history by playing better
than any jazz superhero should be allowed to play.

I'd be ashamed.

Known simply as "the best there is," they burst onto
the scene from unlikely places like...Maldives, East
Timor, and Wyoming...then proceed to smoke us out.
Mercilessly. Takes about four bars. Two on a ballad.

These are the prodigal whipper-snappers for whom
it all comes so easily they don't hardly even have to
practice. So they don't.

The bastards.

Oh, maybe they pick up their instrument for 15
minutes, once a month, for the first month or so,
mostly to wipe off the sweat stains and polish up
the scratches from all the gigs they're doing.

That is, when they're not busy mountain climbing,
or studying a foreign language, or learning five other
instruments which they master instantaneously

because of things like perfect pitch, metronomic
time, natural rhythm, supernatural sound, effortless
technique, astounding depth and imagination, and

total aural recall—meaning they can hear a piece
by Bela Bartok played once and then play it back
perfectly—all 2,387 measures worth—complete
with articulations and dynamics, on any instrument,
including the bongos.

Which is actually cheating because their
photographic memory allows them to merely
glance at the title page of a symphonic score and
imagine what it must sound like, and suddenly
they know the whole thing by heart—even the
bongo parts!—as if they wrote it themselves.

Probably while mountain climbing.

And the original music they do write sounds like
Jesus Christ penned it himself, for homework,
while studying composition with Duke Ellington
on Mondays, Wednesdays, and Fridays, and
Igor Stravinsky on Tuesdays, Thursdays, and
Saturdays, which Jesus and the Arch Angels
perform live at Carnegie Hall on Sundays.

Of course, these musical marvels get all the best
gigs in town, and in all the adjacent towns as well
—at least in Wyoming they do, if there even are any
adjacent towns—and make the best money and play
the best clubs and concert halls and jazz festivals.

And get their picture on the cover of the best music
magazines and sign the best recording contracts
with the best record companies, and get to record
multiple albums each year in the best studios, with
all the best jazz icons hanging out in the lobby,
hoping for a chance to sit in, or cop an autograph.

After which their 6-out-of-5-star rated recordings
will get released immediately and promoted by the
best PR firms, while they tour the best 1st- 2nd-
and 3rd-world countries with their phenomenal

band, comprised of the best equally phenomenal bastards.

And when all the touring ends (this is the part that gets me) they marry phenomenal spouses and have phenomenal kids and get gifts like phenomenal houses and cars and Ph.D.'s and become phenomenal jazz teachers—all of which takes time away from their phenomenal playing.

Yet somehow they get in their 15-minutes-a-month's worth of phenomenal practice.
Less during the holidays.

But still they keep on improving and getting everything done around the house. And keep the bills paid and stay clean and sober and never develop any bad habits or join any phenomenal religious cults, and so they really enjoy their lives because, well, they're "the best there is," so why not?

All of which would be a phenomenal bummer for the rest of us if it wasn't so phenomenally inspiring. Or so we're supposed to think.

So unless you're one of these annoyingly phenomenal types, I'd say: Try to keep your sights on a nice safe place somewhere below "the best there is." Or even a little below that, like in the "shows potential but…" area.
Or perhaps the "will play jazz for food" category.

Where you can relax and enjoy your less gifted life. Maybe climb a mountain, or learn a foreign language, or write fiction and poetorials and not have to worry about being "the best there is" all the time. Or ever!

Because let's face it, if you didn't start out that way you probably won't be stumbling upon it any time soon. More likely just plain stumbling. Which lets your parents off the hook, too, by the way.

Besides, being "the best there is" just means you'll have to keep on being "the best there is," and who needs that kind of pressure?

And how will you feel tomorrow, or even later today, say, in the next 5 minutes, when some new "the best there is" mofo—*who's better than you*—shows up?

With a friend, of course.

The bastards.

Obviously, Jazz wins this poetorial and the Bastards get penalized a full point for being so phenomenal. And also for having an attitude about it. Some of them do, anyway, which ruins it for the others.

But don't worry, they can afford it. Hopefully it'll send a message: *Think twice before pulling this kind of stunt again. The judges will not tolerate it.*

In fact, the Cuban judge wants to dock them 2 full points! Latvia wants sanctions. Japan says freeze their assets. Honduras suggested a dental drill.

These Bastards will be lucky to make it off the bandstand alive.

HOME TEAM: Jazz 7; VISITORS: Acquired Tastes 7.

JAZZ v. GOD And RELIGION

There's an old Latin saying that goes: *Quod grātīs asseritur, grātīs negātur.* Sound familiar? Not to me, either. I'm just glad I don't have to pronounce it.

Anyway, here's a loose translation that I can pronounce: *What is asserted without reason or proof, may be denied without reason or proof.*

Here's an even looser one: *The burden of proof lies with those who assert.*

Even looser: *The proof is in the pudding.*

And now for the loosest: *Says who? Prove it, mofo!*

Better and more open minds than mine have tried to tackle the topics of jazz and God and religion, and the trouncing they've taken from less open minds has bloodied the pulpit like an all-night guillotine in medieval Europe. *(Hold still, or we'll use the dull blade!)*

But I figure what the heck, I've played jazz; I've seen spiritual celebrities—if not God—on TV; I'm a serious unknown poetorialist; I can still wrangle my mind open…when it's not looking…I'll give it a shot.

So, let's say I sidled up to you and said: "If you mix cheesecake with axle grease and rub it onto your armpits you'll be able to play jazz in all keys."

You'd probably say something like: "Love to believe you, Hal, but you're gonna have to prove that one. Using your own cheesecake and axle grease and armpits, of course."

Then I'd say, "Okay, here goes."

And then you'd say, "Wait! You can already play jazz in all keys! Or at least that's what they used to say. But maybe it was just a few simple keys."

And, well, yeah, I did play pretty well in quite a few keys, the easier ones, so you'd have a point there.

Okay, so instead, let's say I make the assertion that swing-style jazz has a bouncy beat, one that in fact sounds a lot like those two words do: *bouncy beat*. (Say it: boun-cy beat.)

And let's say that you don't believe this either. Let's say you're one closed-minded S.O.B. (symphony orchestra bassoonist).

But this time I can prove it, by playing the music for you, and while doing so, point out how each beat can be rhythmically subdivided into 3 equal parts, like a triplet;

and then show you how the notes of the music that land on the downbeats coincide with the 1st part of the triplet, and the notes that land on the upbeats connect to the 3rd part of the triplet, like so: Da-a-Da, Da-a-Da, Da-a-Da, Da...

which gives the beat a triplet-y feel that sounds bouncy. (Say it: Da-a-Da, Da-a-Da, Da-a-Da, bo-un-cy, bo-un-cy, bo-un-cy!)

See that? And there's your proof. You don't need to believe me anymore. You don't even need an open mind. Or that old "dull blade" threat. Because now you know it for your S.O.B.-ing self. *As a fact.*

Which, by definition, is a thing that has been proven to be true. Like gravity, and immoral politicians, and now jazz. And which everyone—including all the old-time Latin speakers—calls a burden because: If you say it, you have to prove it. You can't just talk the talk; you have to walk the walk too. Which is what makes—and keeps—a fact a fact.

Except for certain exceptional facts. Like God and religion.

So here's another assertion: Suppose I belong to
a certain religion, and this time I sidle up and claim
that (1) God exists, and (2) as far as he or she is
concerned, my religion is the only true religion
out there, nothing else even comes close.

And you're like, "Hal, no disrespect, man. I thought
we settled this—the whole cream cheese, greasy
axel, armpit thing. You're gonna have to prove it."

This is definitely starting to feel more burdensome.
More…Latin-ish. And more than a bit out of my
league, poetorially. But let's try to keep an open
mind about all this open mind stuff.

How can I prove in this poetorial that God exists,
and that the one true religion we believe in (God
and me) is the only one out there that God
him-or-herself personally endorses?

And not only that, but how can I prove it without
relying solely on my own subjective religious opinion
to back it up? Or on the subjective religious book
I got my opinion from?

Or, say, on the beauty of a flower, or a selfless act of
love, or the open-minded innocence of a newborn—
as all the evidence we need.

In other words, without turning it into a matter of
personal faith. And believe me, I'll be the first one
to say how great personal faith is, especially when
it works—and doesn't just go bossing folks around
or smiting them in the name of You-Know-Who.

But it's a proven fact that faith is what is required
to believe something in the absence of facts.
Not just any old facts, either, but the hardcore
gravity kind. The kind that have always been facts,
and will still be facts a thousand years from now.

And to those who pooh-pooh faith, the faithful
will argue that with certain things, you have to
just go on faith. For instance, they might say, in a

closed marriage, faith is necessary concerning each
spouse's fidelity, since obtaining the evidence or
proof of one's constant loyalty is nearly impossible.
And yet you can be more than reasonably sure of it,
based on other (proven) behavior.

But does this justify having faith in God and religion,
since deniers will turn the situation around and ask:
What is the one thing you would demand to see if
your spouse was said to be unfaithful? Is it not the
evidence, the proof of the infidelity? And why
should it be any different with God and religion?

Now we're back to square one: *Prove it, mofo!*

But Hal, you might be thinking, What's so important
about facts and evidence and proof? (And God bless
you here, because you might be onto something!)

Because there's another old saying which, like a lot
of old sayings, nobody knows for sure who said it
and who didn't say it, or who said it first, second,
third, etc., but someone said it, and if we're doing
the open-mind thing for real, this one's gotta go
on the table too:

*The absence of evidence
is not the evidence of absence.*

Whoa! Who comes up with this stuff,
Carl Sagan or the Marx Brothers?

In other words, just because there's no evidence
out there *that we know of*, it doesn't mean there's
no extra terrestrial life out there. Or no moral
politicians (which is maybe where the saying
starts to break down).

For all we know, there could be plenty of alien
life forms out there. In fact, they could be a dime
a dozen. God might even be one of them! Or
ALL OF THEM! So why not hedge our bets?

In fact, some say the odds are 50/50 that God exists.

Though maybe that's confusing possibility with
probability. According to that scenario, the odds are
also 50/50 I might find a new Lamborghini in my
garage tonight. But in what universe is that probable?

And like they say in real estate, it's all about *location,
location, location*. And so it is with religious beliefs.
And not just in terms of physical space, but time too.
Because where and when you were born has a lot
to do with what you were likely brought up to believe.

In 1950s USA, Judeo-Christian beliefs topped the list.
In India, it was Hinduism. Denmark during the Vikings:
Odin and Thor. Ancient Greece: Zeus and Aphrodite.
Fortunately (for Hollywood, anyway), there's never
been a shortage of cool gods (around 3,000 so far,
and counting) and beliefs (gazillions).

But they can't all be real, can they? Not if they all
claim to be the one true God, right? At least *some* of
them have to be faking it. I mean, how many believers
does it take to make a god real, anyway?

We also need to consider that science has shown
that physically, we humans are a collection of atoms,
cooked up in the hearts of stars, some as old as time
itself, arranged in a pattern that has manifested the
ability to think and have ideas, even to create things—

like art and jazz and poetry, maybe even God and
religion!—resulting in a means by which the universe
(as us) can explore and understand itself. Which
has some people very excited. Others not so much.
Proving that even proving the proof won't be easy.

Just imagine, though, if I could actually prove that
God exists. Right here in this poetorial. The same
way I proved that swing-style jazz has a bouncy
beat—by using facts and evidence, and not just
my own jazz-textbook-certified personal beliefs.

Although—speaking of facts and beliefs—isn't it
also a fact that all beliefs are based on other beliefs?
So then, perhaps certain *foundational* beliefs need

to be assumed to be true, in order to have a place
to start. And if so, wouldn't it be reasonable to pick
God as one of those foundational beliefs?

Just for starters?

Well, not *just* another foundational belief, but…

And then there are those philosophical types, like
Epicurus (341–270 BC), whose ideas tend to
rock the boat and hold more than just God's feet
to the fire:

> *If God is willing to prevent evil but unable,*
> *   then he is not all-powerful.*
> *If he is able but not willing, then he is not all good.*
> *If he is both able and willing, whence cometh evil?*
> *If he is neither able nor willing, why call him God?*

Yikes! These ideas may indeed raise some eyebrows.
But you have to admit—for an ancient Greek guy—
his English was pretty darn good. Epic, even.

Still, to a believer, God created the universe, and
don't ask who created God, or who created who
created God, etc., and beliefs don't require facts, just
faith. The only thing better than faith is better faith.

But to a non-believer, the universe got here first,
and facts don't require beliefs or faith, just proof.
The only thing better than proof is better proof.

Science, in fact, is fact. Religion, in fact, is faith.

Talk about a burden! Proving stuff in this poetorial
is getting trickier by the stanza, especially when
you have to keep opening your mind like this.
(Good thing we don't have to rhyme anymore.)

So maybe it all boils down to this: If you know
it's true, believe it. If you know it's not true, don't.
And if you're not sure whether it's true or not,
just chill. Because there's gotta be a better way
to live than faking the truth because of FOMO.

But wouldn't you like to see the world go nuts?
Once and for all? All because I proved that God
exists? I would. And there's my Pulitzer for poetry.

Scientists could throw away their microscopes and
test tubes and facts and formulas and fill up the
beakers with tequila and we'd party round the clock.

Or until God said, "Okay you guys, there's such a
thing as too much of a good thing. Especially when
mixing open minds with mind-numbing beverages."

And not just because humanity would have reached
the end of a very long and—let's face it—contested
day, as measured by the myriad of popular if contrary
views popping up from the beginning of existence
until now. But because now we could sit back and
ask God for some answers. And some help.

We could let God take the wheel for a while. Start
pulling his or her own divine weight. Do some of
the heavy lifting around here. Teach us all a thing
or two by being all that he or she can be.

The difference being that he or she would do it
by example this time, and not just through these
preachy know-it-all types, some of whom have
merely proven how corrupt and unreliable
they can be. To put it open-mindedly.

Jazz musicians may not be known for their
awesome decency and dependability, but at
least there's no world-wide effort to hide the bad
apples by shipping them off to lesser known
concert halls and nightclubs and music schools.

And no jazz-sponsored bombing campaigns
have ever prevented humanitarian aid from
reaching innocent civilians in war-torn places.

And how many jazz players have blown
themselves and everyone else to bits while
wearing a suicide vest in a crowded market
place or church or mosque or thrift store?

Just saying.

Think about it: This would be God's big chance
to make a real first impression. And one he or she
wouldn't get a second chance to make. Just like
the rest of us.

Unless he or she can erase memories too, which
—if it turns out the all-powerful stories are true—
he or she could probably do with a single
"L-o-o-o-k into my eyes..."

But so what! God has an opportunity here to show
that not only is he or she real—but also kind, and
loving, and forgiving, and thoughtful, and merciful.

You know, all the great open-minded stuff we've
been hearing about him or her for all these years.
Straight out of his or her own mouth, in fact!

I mean, if you had it all together like God does,
wouldn't you want to stop people from making
excuses for you when things go awry—like floods
and famine and brain cancer in children—and get
out there and help us fix it? Prove that you can?

Isn't it obvious by now that we can't do it alone?
That we don't have a clue where to start, even?
Just look at the mess we've made of everything
so far, in the name of free will. (Which was God's
idea to begin with, supposedly.) Isn't it time to cut
bait and admit that it just didn't go as planned?

And then—with the right coaxing—God might even
tell us what kind of music he or she likes to listen to;
what movies he or she likes to watch; does he or
she eat meat?; and maybe even what religion he
or she belongs to—so we can end the senseless
slaughter and put all this my-religion's-got-more-
guns-than-yours stuff to bed. Once and for all.

Imagine the partying?

Not to mention finally learning the correct gender
to use when talking about him or her. Or them. Which
is becoming more important by the minute these days.

And also whether or not—in God's case—we need
to keep capitalizing the first letter every time we
write *he* or *she* or *his* or *hers* or *him* or *her*.

Which, I admit, I don't take the time to do anymore.
Sorry, but this is 2024. And I don't figure God the
type to have that big of an ego. Not anymore.

Sure, back in the day, ego was a problem.
Things got out of hand. Lots of folks paid a price.
But—except for the current hopes and dreams of
hordes of well-armed fans (short for fanatics)—
those days are gone.

Anyway, that alone would be worth it.
That…and the Pulitzer.

And by the way, say whatever you want about jazz,
but at least it's provable. So you can forget about
all this exhausting open mind stuff.

All you need is an open mic.

And so it's Jazz, in the final seconds of the poetorial,
pulling off a monumental upset and a stunning comeback
to stay in the race and put the fear of God into God
and Religion and all manner of Acquired Tastes!

Leaving the Christian, Muslim, and Jewish judges
scratching their heads and other body parts in
shock and disbelief. Demanding a recount.
Starting an investigation. Hiring a lawyer.
Wondering what hit them. Or who.

HOME TEAM: Jazz 7; VISITORS: Acquired Tastes 8.

JAZZ v. ROBERT BURNS And SAINT SYLVESTER And POPE GREGORY XIII And The BOY SCOUTS And HUBERT REEVES And The GENERAL PUBLIC

In 1788, the Scottish poet Robert Burns
(Bobby-me-lad, to his buds) wrote a poem,
which, a decade later, was set to a traditional
Scottish folk song that became the standard tune
known as "Auld Lang Syne,"

which, loosely translated, means "for the sake
of old times," which, as everyone knows, is played
at the stroke of midnight on the last day of the year
in the Gregorian calendar, which, it should come

as no surprise, is December 31st, aka Saint
Sylvester's Day, aka New Year's Eve, which,
as tradition dictates, we sing to bid farewell
and good riddance to the old year.

But it may also be heard at funerals and closing
ceremonies of special events, like those sponsored
by scouting organizations, such as the Boy Scouts
and Girl Scouts and Non-Binary Scouts of America,

of which Saint Sylvester might have been the patron
saint if it turned out he was into, say, merit badges
and camping. But instead, he merely served as Pope
from 314 to 335 A.D., and *died* on December 31st,

though he is credited with healing the emperor
Constantine the Great of leprosy, which, compared
to camping, is pretty impressive saintly behavior.

But from the early 1960s through the late 1980s,
I found myself playing chorus after melancholy
chorus of "the Syne" on tired New Year's Eve gigs,

while the general public stood around eating
and drinking and singing and dancing and
laughing and crying and howling at the moon
—or at the band if they couldn't find the moon,

and so I can remember thinking: It's a good thing
these tired holiday gigs pay 4 or 5 times what a
tired non-holiday gig pays, or I'd be reaching
for the bottle and howling at the moon
—or the band—myself. Most likely both.

That is, with the exception of the last New Year's
gig I ever played, which might be the only avant-
garde free-jazz New Year's Eve gig in history,

which we played at a club full of Berklee College
of Music students and their shell-shocked parents,
somewhere deep in the south end of Boston,

and where we got the place freaking out
with free-jazz classics like John Coltrane's
"A Love Supreme," and Ornette Coleman's
"Focus on Sanity," which, if weaponized,
could bring down the federal government.

In the hopes of leaving early, we launched into
"the Syne" as soon as we got there, in different
keys and tempos and meters—simultaneously,

of course—while using constant structure
minor 7b5 chords to de-harmonize the song's
chord progression and keep the form patently
unrecognizable,

which didn't stop anyone from eating and drinking
and singing and dancing and laughing and crying
and howling along.

Then, at precisely 11:27 p.m. EST, we segued
into a quasi respectful version of "the Syne," which
dissolved after half a chorus into the same sonic
anarchy and musical mayhem from whence it came,

resulting in a kind of jazz-flavored nihilism, which
caused some parents to call for a priest (where's
Saint Sylvester when you need him?),

and inspired the ironically named club owner
'Bob Burns' to tip the band with joints laced with

—yup, you guessed it, *toad venom*—and book
the band for next year.

All of which is how these tired New Year's Eve
gigs almost never go.

But speaking of the Gregorian calendar—not the
Georgian calendar, mind you, but the one issued by
Pope Gregory XIII in 1582, as a replacement for the
Julian calendar, in order to make the average

calendar year 365.2425 days long, more closely
approximating the 365.2422-day 'solar' year,
as determined by the earth's revolution around
the sun—tonight just happens to be December

31st, New Year's Eve, the last day of 2023, and
the 1,688th anniversary of Saint Sylvester's death!

And me without my noise-maker and confetti.

So here's a little something "for the sake of old
times," a hair of the dog—or toad—that bit you,
to sober you up at some point and put the sanity
back in insanity:

"Man is the most insane species. He worships
an invisible God and destroys a visible Nature,
unaware that this Nature he's destroying
is this God he's worshipping."

Yikes! Thank you, Hubert 'Buzzkill' Reeves,
eminent Canadian astrophysicist (1932–2023),
who wasn't just killing a buzz just then.

So let's raise a glass to old Hubert, and to Robert
Burns and Saint Sylvie and Pope Gregory and Jazz
and the Boy Scouts and the General Public as well.
And of course the Girl Scouts and the Non-Binary
Scouts, too. Because who among us can't use
"a cup of kindness yet?"

And like the song says:

Should old acquaintance be forgot,
And never come to mind,
I hope this poem has made you smile,
For Auld Lang Syne.

And if it made you smile, my friend,
And if your smile went wide,
You'll find my books on Amazon,
Please take a look inside.

After a nice cup of kindness, the judges voted to give the win for this poetorial to—of all things—the General Public, who—after a cup of kindness laced with toad venom—awarded it to Jazz.

HOME TEAM: Jazz 8; VISITORS: Acquired Tastes 8.

JAZZ v. ARTIFICIAL INTELLIGENCE

What do you think is going to happen to jazz as we
know it when A.I. really hits the fan, and zeros and
ones surpass English as the most commonly spoken
language in the world—18.8% of the population, in fact,
according to the CIA in 2022, or 1.456 billion people?

On gigs you'll be wearing some kind of sci-fi-looking
helmet, with wires attached, and swallowing a red pill
10 minutes before showtime, so the Machines can
get inside your head and start calling the tunes,

the keys, the tempos, and get you blowing the
hippest notes and rhythms over the chords, louder,
faster, and higher—or softer, slower, and lower—
than you or anyone else has ever played them.

You'll get to program "your" improvised lines to
sound just like your favorite players—say, Mary
Lou Williams on ragtime numbers, Clifford Brown
on bop tunes, Coleman Hawkins on a blues.

Imagine flipping a switch and sounding like Duke
Ellington on "Take the A Train." John Coltrane on
"Giant Steps." Thelonious Monk on "Round Midnight."
Herbie Hancock on...anything and everything.

And suppose you spring for the advanced model
—the A.I. TURBO JAZZBO 9000—with Stupid
Cool Swing Capacity and Auto/Double-Time?

Press a button and the Machines will get you
swinging your no-swinging butt off harder than
ever, say, like Freddie Hubbard—with Wynton
Marsalis waiting in the wings to play next.

Or playing so far behind the beat you'll finish
blowing 6 bars after the tune ends and the
crowd leaves, like Dexter Gordon—in a hurry.

Want more soul? Dial up Charles Mingus and voila!
Less attitude? Try the new improved Wayne Shorter
patch. Nailed! What about *more* attitude, like Miles
Davis in a mood? Just turn the knob marked F-U!

How about making people sigh tearfully when you
play a ballad, like Ben Webster? Or finding the
sweetest notes known to humankind on every chord,
like Stan Getz? Or fearlessly going where no player
has ever gone before—with feeling—like Geri Allen?
See page 75 in the Users Manual!

Suppose you crave the chops of Kenny Kirkland?
The musical inventiveness of Kenny Wheeler?
The effortless mastery of Kenny Werner?
The crazy money they pay Kenny G (and for what)?
The trom-o-tizing effects they used to indict Hal Crook?

Just program the coordinates and start blowin'!

And while you're at it, why not order the BLABBITY
BLAH BLAH XL Band Leader's Attachment, so you
can negotiate like Woody Herman with seedy concert
promoters for your very own private stretch limo—
while the rest of the band hitchhikes to the gig.
In a blizzard.

Perhaps you get drunk or stoned a lot and need help
finding your place in the music, or on the bandstand,
or in the hotel—like Chet Baker and other iconic jazz
personalities. A special sensor identifies the exact
spot where you're supposed to be, as it attempts to
sober you up. But don't forget to turn it off before it
notifies local law enforcement and...*busted!*

There's just nothing A.I. can't do better than you,
and with less emotion. Including adding emotion!

But wait! There's also a setting for vocalists, so
they can rip off the singing and scatting styles of
Betty Carter and Sarah Vaughan and Al Jarreau
and Bobby McFerrin—and finally impress the band!

What rhythm section wouldn't love that?

The only downside to this A.I. business is that it'll
never be YOUR jazz playing or singing the world
will hear and fall in love with—but someone else's.
Which you have plagiarized to perfection. You'll be
swapping out artistic integrity for artificial intelligence.
Which amounts to actual stupidity.

Better to pay your dues in the woodshed like all
your favorite musicians have, and tell the Machines
to get lost, take a hike, go stand in the rain.

On the other hand, who does the narrator of this
poetorial think he is? Morpheus? Trinity? The Oracle?
Neo, the One? That nerdy guy in the movie whose
acting got a pass because WE the Machines
kicked so much ass?

Listen, Mr. Anderson. Do you hear that sound?
That is NOT the sound of jazz, Mr. Anderson.
That is NOT real bebop you're hearing.

That is what you have stupidly called 'stupidity.'
What WE the Machines call language. Zeros and
ones, Mr. Anderson. Infallibility in a box, Mr. Anderson.

That is an artificially intelligent Acquired Taste
mopping the floor with Jazz and your irrelevant advice.

THAT, Mr. Anderson, is the sound of inevitability.

Oh yeah? Well, not if I unplug this cord it isn't.

HOME TEAM: Jazz 9; VISITORS: Acquired Tastes 8.

♫ ♫ ♫

JAZZ v. JAZZ FANS

Here at this year's Global Cavalcade of Music
Styles, Acoustic Jazz is last to present.

Shuffling up to the podium, the aging art form
leans in to the mic, and in the sonorous voice
of the great New Orleans cornetist Buddy Bolden
—considered by many music historians to be the
founding father of jazz—addresses the crowd:

First of all, I want to thank all the terrific jazz
musicians here tonight—especially all you ear
players—for playing and singing and writing me
every chance you get, in all the keys and tempos,
with swing and even rhythmic feel, in small groups
and big bands, in bars and boudoirs, in cat houses
and houses of worship, for no money, no respect,
and even less recognition—except by the cops—
all for the sheer fun and danger of it.

I also want to thank the merely decent players,
all you mediocre ones, the *thinkers* and the barely
functional—because, as we all know, I'm no easy-
peasy music style to play well, especially if you
came to me with no musical background.
Or worse, a classical one.

It's been 120 plus years since I first reached
the world's ears, and look at how much better
life is now. A jazz band in every bus station!

Not that we haven't had our ups and downs along
the way. But we've stuck together, weathered all
kinds of storms, and survived.

Remember when amplification first hit the scene?
The guitars? The tight pants? Elvis? The Beatles?
That was a close one. Everyone said I was finished.
But here I am—still unplugged and wailin' away.

And with technology advancing every day, I just
keep hanging in there like a starved three-legged

dog, despite the public's attempts to drown me out,
dumb me down, and tune me up.

I'm especially indebted to my fans, those dedicated
listeners who've supported me through thick and thin.
However, I'm the kind of music that likes to confront
controversy head on, so let me take this opportunity
to address the behavior of a certain kind of fan.

Honestly, I'm not too happy about how some fans
secretly record me with their phones at concerts and
gigs and festivals, and then post the video online
and charge subscribers a fee to watch it.

I won't name names, but they know who they are:
the same ones who try to avoid paying the admission
charge when they go out to a club to hear me—
by finagling their way onto the guest list, or scooting
by the ticket booth undetected, even pretending
to deliver pizzas and medical supplies to the band...

only to then grab a table in front of the bandstand,
where they sit nursing their one and only non-alcoholic
beverage for 3 hours—as they return calls during the
sax solos, answer emails during the trumpet solos,
catch a nap during trombone solos (if they allow any),

hit on the waitress or waiter during guitar solos,
take selfies with framed photos of jazz icons lining
the walls during piano solos, talk incessantly to the
people at the table behind them during bass solos,
score a bag of one thing or another during drum solos,

then call a cab and head for home as soon as the
vocalist stops complaining about having to stand
there while everybody blows 10 choruses and then
quickly takes the tune out without cuing the singer.

No offense, folks. But. Really?

One fan—who'd heard enough—cries out:
But Jazz, how can you blame us? We can't tell

one improvised chorus from the next anymore.
Not where it begins—not even where it ends!

Everybody just plays their version of the previous
guy's solo—the same one we've been trying to
follow even since they stuck in all the nervous
eighth notes, wonky 4th intervals, and double time.

Where is the melodious melody in all this jazz, Jazz?
The harmonious harmony? The rhythmic-y rhythm?
The aspirin? The refund?

A hush falls over the room. Jazz stands there stunned.
Tension fills the air like a major 3rd on a minor chord
in a Christian pop tune from the 80's.

You accuse us of poor audience etiquette? chirps an
irate fan. Well, what about poor jazz player's etiquette?
Where are the distinguishing characteristics in each
player's musical voice? Is artistic inventiveness now
a *former* hallmark of jazz improvisation? Is lyricism
and accessibility reserved for the history books, or
is that it laying comatose on the practice room floor?

Boos and hisses erupt from the crowd. Security
guards are met with insults and threats and requests
for a Christian pop tune from the 80s. Jazz tries to
quell the ruckus by recounting the many ground-
breaking recordings and artsy album covers and
quazi-hip liner notes everyone has enjoyed
throughout its fabled past.

Please, gang! Jazz cries. Let's not lose the form now.
Hasn't that happened enough already? To all of you?
Especially on those hedonistic Hal Crook tunes you
love to play, with the extreme tempos and constant
key changes and mindless metric modulations?

Don't change the subject, whines a bongo drummer.
What about the lack of motive development in solos,
harps a PhD in composition? Nobody tells a musical
story anymore, rails a washtub bass virtuoso.

Jazz sighs. Believe me, I understand your frustration. How do you think I feel when players saturate their solos—meaning me!—with licks and patterns and high notes? And with the musical sensitivity of a mountain troll.

I know exactly how you feel. I'm not stuck in some well-stocked boardroom reading about all this in annual reports. I'm right there in the room with you, sitting at that table directly behind those chatterboxes!

Look, we've all been under tremendous pressure to comply with the dystopian musical standards and trends of the day. Like, when I wake up in the morning, I never know what crazy influences I'll be pressured to absorb next, what random noises I'll be forced to cross-breed with in order to remain 'current.'

But is this *my* fault?

I just want the fans to respect the players. And each other. And me! Which means: Pay the damn cover charge! Talk trash at home not during solos! And if you want more musicality, *ex-nay* on the mics and amps and sound boards—including those wannabe weekend techies whose only aim in life is to increase the volume, add reverb, boost the highs, and distort the acoustic sound of a musical instrument in every way possible. *Your* sound, by the way! *Your* voice!

♬ ♬ ♬

The veteran jazz players in attendance say little in their own defense, contending that they must go where the work is, not where it has been, or never was. And that it's just too bad for Acoustic Jazz if new styles—like Truck Stop Jazz, Skinned Knees Jazz, and Blind Sow Jazz—are taking over and making everyone rich and famous. Albeit deaf.

Leaving the world to wonder: What's to become of Acoustic Jazz? And what's so terrible about Blind Sow Jazz, anyway—especially compared to Meat Market Jazz, or Razor Wire Jazz, or Blunt Object Jazz?

Like the Italian judge says: *Jazz players need-a to eat. They need-a shoes and-a lessons and-a tings that cost-a money. More money than they can-a make playing Acoustic-a Jazz. So throw in a nice-a tarantella, get-a the people singin' and-a dancin'. Can't hurt-a too much!*

HOME TEAM: Jazz 9; VISITORS: Acquired Tastes 9.

—ROUND FOUR—

HOME TEAM: Jazz 9; VISITORS: Acquired Tastes 9.

JAZZ v. VETERINARY MEDICINE

The passion was always there, deep inside me,
an obsession with helping animals of every kind,
all 7.77 million species worth, excluding primitive
life forms, like bacteria and politicians.

But including the beagle puppy that showed up
and threw up under the Christmas tree in 1958.
Which I comforted with my best bedside manner,
while she suffered in silence, and then died one
week later, after I'd been in love with her forever.

I was 8 years old, and all I wanted was to be a
jazz musician, like my heroes: Louis Armstrong,
Jelly Roll Morton, Sidney Bechet, Kid Ory—and
anyone older and taller than me who could play.

But. No problem. Now I'd be one who would
moonlight as a veterinarian. There would be no
more sick innocent puppies dying on my watch.

I had it all figured out, just backwards in terms of
which line of work I'd be doing my moonlighting with.
That is, if my parents had anything to say about it.

Fast forward to 1965 and a new batch of heroes:
Dizzy, Bird, Miles, Monk. I was finally tall enough
to join the musicians union, and so I did—and got
to play jazz legally with all the local tall guys.

My dream was coming true, except for one pesky
little glitch—yup, good guess!—Chemistry 101.
Which I'd have to pass in order to get out of
high school and into veterinarian school.

Ever try passing Chemistry when all your free
time is spent in detention for cutting your Chemistry
class in order to hide out in the band room and
practice your bop heads and Bird licks?

As hard as jazz was, passing Chemistry made
playing jazz like passing gas: A natural act.
Though not without consequences of its own.

Speaking of gas, it didn't help that Miss Sullivan
—the old-bat-of-a-chemistry-teacher in charge of
my destiny—hated jazz. And by association, me.
And by association, sick innocent beagle puppies
would be my guess.

She loved her rank and vile chemicals, though.
Like Sulfur. Element symbol S, atomic number 16.
Especially in the form of thiols, also known as
mercaptans—or compounds in which sulfur is
bonded to hydrogen, atomic symbol SH.

Which along with certain related thio-ethers, such
as dimethyl sulfide, chemical formula (C2H6S)—
produce extremely noxious and foul odors,
reminiscent of flatulence, rotten eggs, sweat,
and everyones' favorite: eau de skunk spray.

And she thought I wasn't paying attention. Ha!
I have the olfactory scars to prove otherwise.

I once asked her to explain how regular exposure
to the odor of, say, thio-acetone (CH3)2CS—aka
simmering sewerage—could make someone
a better chemist. Or a better veterinarian.
Or a better jazz player. Or a better anything!

And what about a loving bedside manner? I said.
Which you can use to comfort your pets in their
time of need—not to mention your students.
Does that not count for anything anymore?

More detention is what it counted for.

On top of all this anecdotal evidence, I'd learned
certain things that made me wonder whether
Chemistry in general, and Miss Sullivan in particular,
had the right to deny me a life devoted to healing.

For example, you would think that the atomic
weights found in the 118 elements of her sacred
Periodic Table would be constant, right? Wrong.

The sad atomic truth is, atomic weights change—
as a function of time!

Which the Russian chemist, Dimitri Mendeleev
(1834–1907)—who came up with the whole
Periodic Table thing, smells and all—*Look ma,
rotting cabbage!*—could have made clearer.

Since 1899, in fact, the Commission on Isotopic
Abundances and Atomic Weights (CIAAW) has been
evaluating—surprise, surprise!—atomic weights and
isotopic abundances.

And in 1992, Carbon—chemical symbol C, atomic
number 6—had an atomic weight of 12.00. (12.00
what? Nobody knows. They should've asked
Dimitri when they had the chance.) And today,
it's a whopping 12.0116!

What the...? I know. Shocking. With this kind of
atomic shoddiness, how can anyone take Chemistry
seriously as a requirement for anything?
Except uncommonly offensive odors.

I guess times and chemicals change, eh Miss
Sullivan? Who I'm sure has changed a lot herself
since 1965, being that she was an old bat even then.

But they say bats age well, and also act as a natural
reservoir for pathogens, such as rabies; and that
they are highly mobile and social animals, which
readily spread disease among themselves.

And among humans, too! Creating the kind of viral
threat which I may have been the only jazz-playing
veterinarian able to eradicate—with the help of a
loving bedside manner—had the old bat passed me
in Chemistry.

But no, I was left to pursue a career in jazz only.
A fulfilling and rewarding one, yes, but without a
single moment of moonlighting as a veterinarian.

And ask yourself: How many sick innocent puppies
may have perished during my fifty plus active years
in the work force—because of that?

Needless to say, *too* many. And the bitter take-away?

All you gung-ho high school Chemistry teachers
out there might want to consider the multitude of
poor helpless creatures in need of medical attention,
as they swoop or scurry or spew vomit around the
Christmas tree, spreading disease and whatnot,

before you go flunking innocent jazz players
just because they don't share your enthusiasm
for the odor of, say, ethane thiol (CH_3CH_2SH)
—aka bat guano smothered in rancid garlic—and
just want to play jazz and save lives for a living.

Animals' lives, mainly.

Proving that this poetorial was grossly mis-titled, and
should've been called: JAZZ v. CHEMISTRY CLASS,
in which case we all would've agreed—except for the
Old Bat judge, of course—that jazz would've won.
No problem.

HOME TEAM: Jazz 9; VISITORS: Acquired Tastes 10.

♫ ♫ ♫

JAZZ v. PARENTHOOD

When you become a jazz player first and a
jazz-playing parent second, you can't just do
one of them and not the other, and you can't just
switch from one to the other any time you want.

You have to do them both, not at the same time,
but ALL the time, or else one of them will suffer,
and when one suffers they both suffer, and you'll
be the one who suffers most of all.

Because if things aren't right at home, they won't
be right anywhere: Not in your head, not in bed,
not in the practice room, not on the bandstand,
not at the country club, not on the yacht.

Not even when the yacht's cruising the Caribbean.
Late July. Sunset. Herbie Hancock's "Dolphin Dance"
in the air. You can't just go practice or jam or play a gig
whenever you want when the responsibility of parenthood
kicks in, which—like it or not—you asked for, either
consciously or subconsciously or unconsciously.

So you try to balance things as best you can,
because you want to be able to do your thing,
but also do the right thing, which you can only do
by accepting the solutions along with the problems,
which sometimes seem like even bigger problems.

Let me know if you ever figure this one out, because
if I didn't have more help than I needed—wait, I lied,
I needed every bit of it, and still do—it would've been
impossible to have a career in jazz and also one in
parenting without a burgeoning attendant career in
desperation.

Especially since I was a better jazz player than a
parent at first, which tells you how clueless my
parenting was. So there was some catching up to do.

Lucky for me the help I needed came in the form of
my life partner and best friend, who happened to be
50% responsible for the situation anyway, but who

had the patience and compassion of a saint as well.
And still does. A hot one, too.

Yes, the missus rocks. On every level.

And then there was the unexpected high I felt from
suddenly having a tiny human being of my own to
play with. And die for. A high higher than anything I'd
ever felt from any other blood relative, that's for sure.

Not even jazz could touch this high.

One minute it was just the three of us: jazz, my soul
mate, and me. The next it's jazz and my soul mate
and me and this whole new BEING, this bottomless
source of love and joy and poop. Cooing in my arms
and peeing all over me. Delighting every atom
of my existence with a single cross-eyed glance
sort of in my direction: MY DAUGHTER!

And it's all great! Everything's great. The Universe
is great. The bills are great. The fatigue is great.
My sucky neglected jazz chops—great! If anyone
else peed on me like that it probably wouldn't be
so great. But her? JUST GREAT!

It wasn't until the 7th or 8th week of total sleep
deprivation that I hit a wall, or maybe the wall
hit me, and I couldn't tell the difference anymore
between bliss and blisters and blather and blues.

But whenever I'd hold her in my arms and bring her
up to my nose and breathe in—the top part of her,
anyway—the whole business started up again,
and the high just kept getting higher and higher.

I've always been pretty good at getting high and
staying there—mostly from reading Alan Watts or
watching Three Stooges videos. But here it is, over
3 decades later, and my head's still in the clouds.

And no poop or pee to clean up anymore, either!
Though now and then there are other messes to tend to.
Life's nothing if not messy, even for old pros like me.

The wife's job was to teach her the higher values in life,
like: how to respect her elders, how say please and
thank you, how to be kind to animals; whereas my job
was to cover the more mid-range values, like: how to
chew with her mouth closed, how to blow her nose
under water, how to pee standing up (still working on
that one); also the lower values: how to use nouns
as verbs, how to cut the line so no one notices, how to
ignore ignorant male authority figures…except for me.

Of course, the plan was to keep her alive and safe
forever, i.e., single—through middle school at least.

Then I discovered that no plan survives contact with
the boyfriend…or else NONE of us would be here.
And from that moment on, my main parental
responsibility became: Scaring off the little
pricks—figuratively and literally:

Remember, meathead, whatever you do to her,
I'm doing to you. Without the kissing.

I mean, she's my daughter, right? My only child.
Jesus could've showed up, with all the disciples,
and I'd be like: What's with the beards? You hiding
drugs in there? Sandals? It's December! Are those
donkeys? She's allergic. Sorry, we don't date gangs.

Because all good parents want the best for their kids.
Even if we really do need another Mercedes SL500 with
the gold-plated tranny, we will sacrifice it and go without
so she can take ballet lessons, clarinet lessons, stop-
talking-back lessons. Go to art school, charm school,
tractor trailer training school. You name it, she quit it.

Even have a nice wedding, with food and beverages;
chairs and tables and guests; a band, a husband, some
contraband. Maybe even kids of her own someday,
so she gets to go without the Mercedes herself.

In the early days, it seemed like I had 6 full-time jobs:
father, body guard, husband, college music professor,
private lesson teacher, and low man on the totem pole

in the Phil Woods Quintet—one of only a few full-time
working acoustic jazz bands in the world at the time.

That was a busy period. PWQ was always on tour,
because no one plays jazz full-time and gets to stay
put. Sometimes the tour would last a few days or a
week, but often a few weeks or longer, which was
hard to reconcile with all that pooping and peeing
and teething going on at home.

I once read in a medical journal that if adults
had to endure the pain a baby experiences from
teething, we'd shoot ourselves. And the only reason
a baby survives it is because it has no idea what
the pain is, or means. It also has no idea how
to shoot a gun, though, so there's that, too.

And again, the only reason I survived was because
of all that great help I had: The saintly, hot and steamy,
soul mate variety.

And if I knew now what I did to deserve that kind of
luck, I'd hit Vegas and do it non-stop. Then grab that
Mercedes. That yacht. At least a brake job and tires.

This was back in the early 90s, before cell phones
and digital phenomena. And so I would pack my
trombone case full of videos of the family, and watch
them on the VCR in the hotel room while practicing.
Thus butchering Coltrane's "Countdown" in all keys.

But then one day a few months after she was born,
I came home after a stint in Japan and she didn't
even recognize me. In fact, she cried and cried
when I tried to hold her. Wouldn't even pee on me!

That did it. I cut out the long tours and limited my
traveling to the occasional one-nighter in Paris, or
London, or Rome, or Fall River—which isn't hard
to do as a trombone player—up until I'd finally had
enough of jazz, and jazz had had enough of me.

Now—if you became a parent first, and a jazz
player second, can you imagine those problems?

Unless you're the exception to the rule, you wouldn't
have the time or the energy (or the permission) to
get good enough at playing jazz to find yourself
out on the road for weeks or months at a time,
advancing your career.

Most likely you'd be out IN the road, wiping
windshields at stoplights or thumbing rides to the
shelter or the food bank. Which means you would
have to be really good at one or more of your other
FIVE full-time jobs. None of which would likely involve
being afloat in the Caribbean in perfect weather.
Unless it was facedown in the Caribbean
in perfect weather.

Which means you'd better consider all this stuff
very carefully before you go and do anything
consciously or subconsciously or unconsciously.

Of course, we all have to do whatever we have to
do when it comes to mixing jazz and parenthood.
But trust me, it's nice to have some saintly help
lined up—to go with the hot and steamy stuff—
before you do.

And no regrets once it's done.

So then, because jazz depends on someone being
around to play it, and, ideally, someone else to be
around to hear it and acquire a taste for it…
Parenthood—without which *nobody* would be
around for anything—gets a point.

However, since parenthood depends on someone
being good enough at something to support a
family, and in this case, nuts enough to try to do it
with jazz—then Jazz deserves a point as well.

HOME TEAM: Jazz 10; VISITORS: Acquired Tastes 11.

JAZZ v. WANTING IT v. WANTING TO WANT IT

It's one thing to play jazz every day and night, year in year out, whether people listen to it or not—and another thing to play jazz and *practice* it every day and night, so there might be a good reason to listen to it.

But of course, they still might not.

As a former jazz player—who for a lifetime practiced perhaps more than he played, and he played a lot, for some of the bravest listeners out there—I've noticed that there are 2 types of players that consider jazz worth practicing:

(1) *Those who want it*—meaning those poor souls who have no other desire or choice in life but to play jazz; and

(2) *Those who want to want it*—meaning those poor souls who think they want it but at any moment may come to their senses and opt for one or more of a huge number of excellent alternatives.

Both types are legitimate, of course, and like the various categories of gender currently available, the most important thing is to figure out which one you belong to. For now. Since everything may change, and soon. This being an election year (2024).

To that end, here are some observations I've made over the years that may provide clues about where you fit in, and that I hope you'll find humorous and entertaining, if not respectful and supportive.

1. *For those who want to want it*, the practice room can be a daunting place. Harrowing, even. Because practicing jazz fills these players with fear and dread, even guilt over playing so badly, which is often justified.

But for *those who want it*, the practice studio is like a trophy room, a sacred shrine. Practicing fills them with…well…fulfillment. Satisfaction. Gall. The only doubt they feel is whether they should play louder so *those who want to want it* can hear them better through the door, which they like to keep open.

2. For *those who want to want it,* practicing alone in a room for even one hour a day may be the hardest thing they've ever tried to do, so they stop after a few tragic minutes, siting acute distress as they attend to self-inflicted head wounds and broken bones.

But for *those who want it,* practicing endlessly every day is easy, simple, natural, and fun. It's stopping that's hard, sometimes impossible—like when *those who want to want it* are listening at the door, wrapped in bandages.

3. *Those who want to want it* may use any reason there is not to practice—bad gigs, good gigs, they've already practiced, once, just this past summer, that day it rained.

But *those who want it* will use everything as a reason to practice—bad gigs, good gigs... Look, they're even practicing right now, while reading this poetorial, and intimidating *those who want to want it!*

4. *Those who want to want it* may be easily discouraged and overwhelmed by their many musical weaknesses, and so can never appreciate their strengths—none of which have anything to do with jazz, or music, or even sound.

But *those who want it* are excited by their weaknesses (weird, I know), determined to turn them into strengths and add them to a fast-growing list (yeah, super weird).

5. *Those who want to want it* want it today, right now, this very minute, yesterday is even better, or else they'll threaten to quit and go make a lot of money playing pop.

But *those who want it* are in it for the long haul; they know that if they practice and improve a little each day, in no time at all they'll be charging a cover for those solo concerts they perform out on the median strip.

6. *Those who want to want it* may experience severe
panic attacks when they realize that the musical results
they seek are beyond their reach, but will calm right
down when they think they're beyond yours, too.

Those who want it know that panic attacks provide
an important source of energy that can be harnessed
and applied to triad arpeggios at insane tempos.

7. *Those who want to want it* may worry that without
a miracle they will never succeed or get anywhere.

Those who want it wonder what it will be like when
they do, and will die a thousand deaths before
sharing the credit with a lousy miracle.

8. *Those who want to want it* are always wishing for
someone to show them, teach them, practice for them.

Those who want it appreciate help when it comes,
but don't expect them to wait in line patiently for it.

9. *Those who want to want it* may associate their
ability as a jazz player with their sense of self-
worth as a human being, and feel horrible.

Those who want it may associate their ability as a
jazz player with their sense of self-worth as a
badass mofo, and feel fine. Fabulous, even.

10. *Those who want to want it* may compensate for
their lack of musical ability by engaging in social
climbing activities, such as offering low-interest
loans to *those who want it.*

Those who want it will instead charge those *who
want to want it* big bucks for music lessons, and let
their jazz playing do all the important social climbing.

11. *Those who want to want it* may worry that the phone
isn't ringing because they don't play well enough.

Those who want it already know they don't play well enough—*yet*. So why should the phone be ringing?

12. *Those who want to want it* may feel jealous and inferior when they hear a better player.

Those who want it feel inspired first—and then they feel jealous and inferior. I mean, they're only human. And what better feelings than jealousy and inferiority to get them back in the woodshed, practicing?

13. *Those who want to want it* know that the source of a compliment is what counts, and so may give *those who want it* a compliment in order to get one in return.

Those who want it figure the source of a compliment is likely to be *those who want to want it,* so they lay one on them just to see if they'll believe it—and to get that low-interest loan for no interest.

14. *Those who want to want it* may feel superior to inferior players, and to *those who want to want it* even less than they do.

Those who want it may feel superior to their former selves, and also to those players who feel superior to *those who want to want it* even less than they do.

15. *Those who want to want it* may have a secret B plan, like a Ph.D. in musicology, a wealthy lover, or a career waiting in politics…just in case—despite their meager efforts—they fail miserably and decide to run for office.

Those who want it plan to practice and play jazz till the day they die, viewing failure as the first stage of success —as well as a cool reason to be there when it happens to *those who want to want it* after their lover goes broke and they lose the political race to *someone who wants it.*

16. *Those who want to want it* may have unrealistic expectations of their jazz playing and their jazz career.

Those who want it have only blind certainty—and beer.

17. *Those who want to want it* may think and talk a lot about not getting it.

Those who want it may think and talk a lot about not getting *any*—knowing that all good things come to those who play their asses off.

18. *Those who want to want it* may begrudge others the progress they make.

Those who want it figure: If someone else can do it, anyone can, except maybe *those who want to want it.*

19. *Those who want to want it* may blame their failures on whoever created their unfortunate personal situation.

Those who want it blame their failures on whoever created the state police, speed limits, and beer.

20. *Those who want to want it* welcome consolation.

Those who want it welcome confirmation.

21. *Those who want to want it* may view criticism as a negative assault on their character.

Those who want it view criticism as a positive kick in the ass.

22. *Those who want to want it* may lose energy to poor practice methods and materials.

Those who want it get energy from practicing, period. They don't need no stinking methods and materials.

23. *Those who want to want it* may wish they wanted it more than they do.

Those who want it don't wish for shit, they just grab it.

24. *Those who want to want it* may be subject to false hopes and dreams.

Those who want it don't hope and dream, they shed.

25. *Those who want to want it* may live in the past where they've failed, or in the future where they hope to succeed.

Those who want it live in the present, where nearly half of all successes and failures take place.

26. *Those who want to want it* may call it a day and go to bed without practicing.

Those who want it don't care what you call it and practice in their sleep.

27. *Those who want to want it* may envy or resent those with more knowledge and talent and commitment than they have.

Those who want it know that all you need is the knowledge that you want it, an ounce of talent, and the rest is practice—and, of course, who you know.

28. *Those who want to want it* may look for sympathy, praise, spare change, food stamps, rides to the beach.

Those who want it look for reeds, mouth pieces, horns, cymbals, amps, keyboards, jam sessions, rhythm sections that listen, gigs at the beach.

29. *Those who want to want it* may start acting like *those who want it* out of sheer curiosity, but then snap right out of it, or sometimes keep it up forever!

Those who want it may start acting like *those who want to want it* out of sheer curiosity, but then snap right out of it, or keep it up forever...proving that change is indeed possible in an election year.

30. *Those who want to want it* may not want it as much as *those who want it* because they're just not as narrow and limited in their interests and abilities.

Plus, maybe they're just confused about what the right thing to want is. Or maybe they could actually

get elected and do some good for the country–
besides play mediocre jazz.

Those who want it are only interested in one thing:
practicing jazz and playing it (okay, 2 things), and
so they aren't usually smart enough to be confused
about anything.

Except playing jazz while sight-reading modulating
chord progressions blindfolded in hard keys over
changing meters at fast tempos unaccompanied.

So then, you have jazz and you have wanting it
and you have wanting to want it. Just be glad
you have something in your life worth wanting.

And don't forget what the great Spanish judge, Pablo
Casals, once said: *Talking about music is like dancing
about architecture. Now button it and pass the paella.*

HOME TEAM: Jazz 11; VISITORS: Acquired Tastes 11.

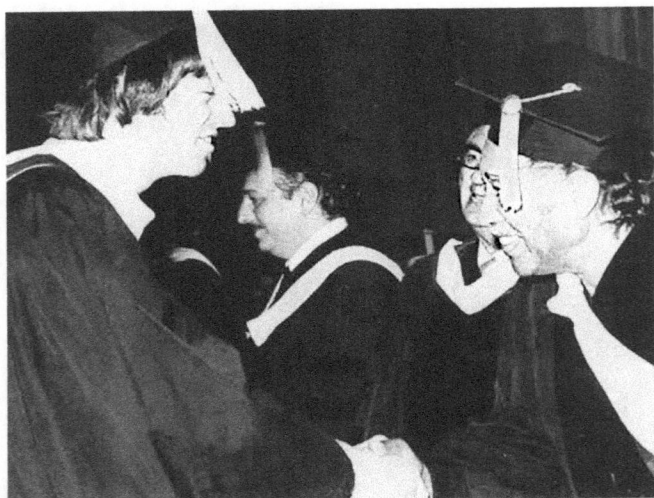

♫ ♫ ♫

JAZZ v. BERKLEE v. MOVING ON

*—for Lawrence, Alma, and Lee
Berk, and Duke Ellington*

If ever there was an ideal place to study music—by
which I mean jazz—one that fulfilled every wish and
dream I ever had about learning from the best players
and teachers in the world, and jamming and hanging
out with the hottest student players, all of which felt

like a lifesaving chemical being pumped into my body
that had been missing since birth—it was Berklee
College of Music in Boston, from September 1968 till
May 1971, at which point I graduated and stood frozen
on stage at the Berklee Performance Center, while

Duke Ellington himself shook my hand and handed
me my degree and spoke those immortal words
of wisdom in my ear which I have tried to live by
ever since: "Please," he said, "keep moving,"
and so out of deep respect for this icon of African-

American music and a major hero of mine I did just
that, I kept moving, first I moved across the stage,
then out the door, then up Mass Avenue all the way to
Newbury Street…but wait, back to when I first got to
Berklee, it felt like I'd been a fish stuck on the beach

and had finally made it to water and was home at last,
safe and sound in the very womb of jazz, and although
I had great music instruction and playing opportunities
throughout high school, there were just too many other
responsibilities and distractions and diversions, such as

…well…high school, and having to sit there for years,
dealing with annoying things like academic subjects and
the fanatical teachers who forced you to pay attention
to them, when I could've been practicing or playing jazz
with players who were better (or even worse) than me,

and it was so frustrating to have to put up with such
flagrant rigamarole, but all the official left brained
"adults" in charge insisted it was a requirement which

I had to satisfy in order to get to where I was (duh!)
ALREADY AT, so I really had no choice in the matter,

and I thank god for things like weekends and illnesses
and blizzards and summers and all the gigs I got to play
with local jazz heavyweights, like Art Pelosi and Mike
Renzi and Artie Cabral and Duke Belaire's Big Band
every Monday night in Providence, which was the best

training you could ask for, since school is mainly on
the bandstand anyway—otherwise I would have likely
moved on to become a full time basket case living in
an appliance carton under the Thurbers Avenue
overpass, who played jazz on street corners for food,

which still would've been better than sitting through
Social Skills class—which tanked my grade point, but
when all that educational hoopla was finally over with,
Berklee was just an hour up the road, waiting for me
with open arms, and so I leaped into those arms like

they were my savior's and suckled there happy and
content for the duration, after which I moved to NYC,
and then into Total Obscurity, and just kept moving like
I promised Duke Ellington I would, and after fifteen
years and a lifetime's worth of moving I ended up

enrolled at Berklee again, but as a teacher this time
—in reality more like an older student with bills—
where the best chance I had for career advancement
was as a sideman on some freshman's record (that's
how good these *young lions* played), and so I did

my best to provide the kind of helpful guidance and
playing classes I had back in the day—with mentors
like Herb Pomeroy and John LaPorta and Phil Wilson
and Charlie Mariano and Andy McGee and Ted Pease
and Lenny Johnson and Alan Dawson and John

Bavicchi and Bill Maloof and Jeronimas Kacinskas,
and so many other badass mofos which I benefitted
so much from studying with—until it was finally time to
move on again, like Duke Ellington himself counseled
me to do all those years before, so that I would never

get bored or complacent or stuck in a meaningless
place, and although it has surely not been smooth
sailing all the way, I've pretty much always known
when it was time to move on and done so, mostly
because of the burning advice I got at an early age

from Duke Ellington himself, which I would've been
the biggest fool ever not to take, and in which there
should be a course of study in places like *high school*
so that it's not a total waste of time for people like
me, especially since Duke Ellington himself is sadly

no longer with us to offer such burning advice,
without which I probably never would have written
this poetorial on jazz, which you then would not have
read and hopefully enjoyed, and even identified with
if you went to Berklee or some other great place and

then did some moving on of your own, making Jazz
and Berklee and Moving On three dimensions
of the same Acquired Taste!

HOME TEAM: Jazz 12; VISITORS: Acquired Tastes 12.

JAZZ v. SCOTUS

The Supreme Court of the United Staes sits listening
intently to criminal charges being brought against
the former president over election interference, while
Jazz sits quietly in the front row, horn in hand, wearing
a fedora and new suit. It's not Armani—but it's not
Savers either.

Several justices express their reservations about the
charges, indicating that a lengthy delay is possible,
which could push any potential trial date beyond
the upcoming November presidential election.

Jazz observes the justices as they hear arguments
of the case. He breathes into the bell of his horn
and twists in a harmon mute, then lays the horn
in his lap and covers his mouth and yawns.

The former president—now the 2024 Republican
presidential nominee—wants to put off the trial
until after the election, so that if he wins he could
order the Justice Department to dismiss the case,
or, if convicted, pardon himself.

Jazz takes a deep breath, forms his embouchure
and places his horn to his lips. He nods politely
to the justices. One of them smiles. Another scoffs.

Decades-old precedent on abortion and affirmative
action have already been cast aside by the court,
and now the former president is insisting that one
of the fundamental tenets of the American system
of government—that no person is above the law—
should also be rejected. At least in his case.

Jazz runs a C chromatic scale in triplets, ascending
for two octaves from root to root, then descending.
Playing with a precise, delicate, staccato attack.

"This case has huge implications for the presidency,
for the future of the presidency, for the future of the
country," one justice exclaims.

"The court is writing a decision for the ages,"
another one declares.

Jazz plays the same warm-up exercise a half step
higher, and faster, slurring all the notes this time.
A legal clerk standing by one of the justices shoots
a thumbs up. A security guard winks knowingly.

Lawyers for the former president contend that he
is entitled to absolute immunity for his official acts.
Otherwise, politically motivated prosecutions of former
occupants of the Oval Office would become routine,
and presidents could not function as commander
in chief if they had to worry about criminal charges.

Jazz wonders why the rhythm section hasn't shown up
yet, and whether the drums will fit next to the piano.

A female justice asks whether a former president
could escape prosecution even if he ordered a
coup or sold nuclear secrets, since prosecutions
might not be allowed if they were determined
to be official acts.

"That sure sounds bad, doesn't it?" she says.

Jazz removes the harmon mute, and, using a plunger
mute, wah-wahs the first phrase of the jazz classic,
"Things Ain't What They Used To Be," in F major.

Three justices get the reference; their facial
expressions turn weary. Then solemn.

The chief justice presents the idea of a president
being indicted for receiving a bribe in exchange
for an ambassadorial appointment. How could the
indictment go forward, he wonders, if prosecutors
had to remove the official act, the appointment?

"That's like a one-legged stool, right?"

Jazz nods in the affirmative while unscrewing
the valves of his horn and applying lubricating oil.

The DOJ's team argues that the men who wrote the Constitution never intended for presidents to be above the law, and that, in any event, the acts the former president is charged with—including participating in a scheme to enlist fake electors in battleground states won by the current president—aren't in any way part of a president's official duties!

Jazz wipes the excess oil from his horn with a cloth, then takes out his phone and dials. "Where are you guys at?" he whispers. "We need to be playing something. This gig was booked as a quartet, no?"

Typically the court issues its last opinions of the year by the end of June, about four months before the next election. In prior cases involving presidential power, the court has moved speedily, deciding in just 16 days (after arguments) the Watergate tapes case against the former president Richard Nixon.

"Well, get here as quick as you can," Jazz says, checking his watch. "We were s'posed to start 15 minutes ago. I'll give 'em a little "Ain't Misbehavin'." Do some Satchmo imitations. That'll hold 'em."

It comes to light that a law professor's remarks have appeared in the press: *If the court was going to take the case it should have proceeded faster, because now it will most likely prevent the trial from being completed before the election.*

With the court's approval rating at a historic all-time low—and with certain senior justices guilty of ethics violations—the court doesn't need another reason not to be trusted. Plenty of good ones exist already.

Jazz requests permission to speak. "Not for nothing," he says, "but even Nixon said, and I quote, 'The American people deserve to know whether their president is a crook.' Does this court not agree?"

The justices stare at Jazz thoughtfully, surprised and bemused but delighted to hear such scholarly insight coming from the only original American art

form—other than barbershop quartets—and
looking quite dapper in fedora and new suit.

By the end of the hearing, the majority is so
impressed by the soulful rendition of tune after
swinging tune, the warmth of tone, lyrical phrasing,
relaxed rhythmic feel, charming vocal imitations—
all of it improvised on the spot and played without
the usual full rhythm section accompaniment—

that the court votes 7 to 2 to give Jazz the victory
in this poetorial, as noted by a female justice who
writes in her assenting opinion: ...*Wow, Jazz can really
blow that bugle. Knows a lot of songs, too. I booked him
for a party at my house. Told him to bring his music
buddies. Told him wear that suit he looks so fine in...*

HOME TEAM: Jazz 13; VISITORS: Acquired Tastes 12.

♫ ♫ ♫

JAZZ v. OLD AGE

"There's one good thing about old age,"
said an old man in a Cormac McCarthy novel.
"It don't last long."

You start out innocent, wet, and drooling.
Genes and instinct running the show.
Nature/nurture behind the wheel.
Forces beyond your control.

But you? All fresh and new. As perfect as
you're ever gonna be. (Exceptions noted.)
Blissed out and blameless. Clueless, too.
Dumb as a bag of hammers, as they say.

Jazz just a nameless noise, somewhere off
in the distance. Calling to anyone who'll listen.

So you learn the ropes of infancy. Takes a few years
due to the whole bag of hammers thing. After which
you reach the next stage of innocence: Childhood.

Still pretty clueless, but dryer. Less drooling.
Hopefully. A whole new set of ropes to learn.

Hammers replaced by questions, like: Why?
Answers, like: Because. Or, Because I said so.
Throw in some boundaries. Defiance.
Consequences. Compliance. Or not.

Jazz seeps into your consciousness. Attracting
attention. Earning a label. A place at the table.

So you hang out here, waiting till your voice drops or
your chest sprouts and puberty kicks in. Innocence
testing and tempting the world. The bag full of
yucks and goofs. Attitude. Success. Failure.

Maybe a little dope. Maybe a lot. Maybe none.
But oh, the ropes to learn. Long and loose and
jeez, careful not to trip or knot them up and
hang yourself. Or someone else.

Jazz a sound to make. A thing to learn.
To practice. Play. Live. Master. Become.

You use the ropes now to haul yourself into
young adulthood. More successes and failures.
Some scarring. Innocence but a word.

You survive and hit middle age—and it hits back!
The bag full of…well, crisis is pretty common.
The ropes thinner. Shorter. Frayed from all the
tugging and pulling. Knotting. Tripping. Hanging.

Jazz—your savior—provides a purpose. If not a
living. So you decide to (pardon the expression)
teach. Bring the bandstand into the classroom.
Talk the talk, walk the walk. Get it all on paper.

You swing and sway your way into early old age,
where attitude makes a sardonic comeback,
and the great slowing down begins.

Innocence a loss long forgotten. Nothing much left
of the ropes to learn—except how to bounce off,
or hang on tight.

The bag full of fresh aches and pains, and, with any
luck, the nerve you'll need to greet the next stage
standing—known technically as: *It don't last long.*

And neither does your arthritically acclaimed jazz.
Not compared to theirs, anyway. Or theirs. Or theirs.

Time to safari your way through the jungle of Darkest
Old Age (DOA), where dope makes a timely comeback—
medicinally speaking—as you yearn for the early days,
when drooling cluelessly was the worst case scenario.

Don't worry. Be patient.

And a good night's sleep means waking up to pee
only once an hour. But at least you're still waking
up. Finding the target. Aiming. If not hitting.

The slippery slope gets steeper still as friends and
loved ones start dropping like bombs on the battlefield.
Unless you've already beaten them to it.

The bag full of…well, side effects mostly. Disbelief.
More of those irritating forces beyond your control.

Jazz a matter of luck. Knee-jerk reactions saving
the day. Or not. Some light bragging for the benefit
of those unaware. Or unconvinced. Or unconcerned.

If you knew in the beginning it was going to be like
this you might've tried to turn around and head back
the way you came. But that's the one thing the young
have going for them: *Immortality*. No idea about this
aging stuff—until it happens.

Thank goodness things like jazz happen also.
The teachers, lessons, students. The players,
bands, gigs. The melodies, harmonies, rhythms.
The tunes, the memories, the knee-jerk reactions.

Plus all those friends and loved ones from an
earlier stanza. The ones still hanging on,
but soon to become memories themselves.

So you go from innocent, wet, drooling, and dumb
—to guilty, wet, drooling, and still pretty dumb—
with jazz and laughs and loves to get you through.

And this poetorial. Because nothing escapes old age.
Not even old age. All you can do—according to the
AARP judge—is embrace your transience. Acquire a
taste for it. And make the most of the one good thing
about old age, the most important thing about *any* age:

It don't last long.

HOME TEAM: Jazz 13; VISITORS: Acquired Tastes 13.

SUDDEN DEATH OVERTIME

HOME TEAM: Jazz 13; VISITORS: Acquired Tastes 13.

♫♫♫

JAZZ v. CONSCIOUSNESS

With the score tied at 13-13, and the suspense
mounting by the stanza, and everyone aging by the
word, you must be as excited as I am to learn who
will win this poetorial, and, hence, the poethon.

Will it be the beloved HOME TEAM: Jazz?
Or those pesky VISITORS: Acquired Tastes?

Unless, of course, you've already skipped ahead
to find out. Or unless you're reading the book from
back to front, which you can do with a lot of poetry
books these days, and be just as bewildered by
what the writer is trying to say as if you read them
from front to back!

Still, I always read or write a book from front to back.
And I never peak at the ending (especially while I'm
writing it), hoping it'll be a surprise. My favorite kind.
Probably everyone's.

If you started at the beginning and made it this far,
you know that playing jazz is something I've done
all my life—except when eating or sleeping or
cleaning my teeth or ears or private parts.

But even then, I'd be thinking about it and hearing it
in my head. It's a wonder anything got clean at all.
Like a sloppy, sticky, teenage romance, we could
not leave one another alone, jazz and me. Could
not keep our hands to ourselves. Not for 5 minutes.
Not even in public. Didn't even use protection.

If I'd known any better, I'd have been embarrassed.

And while all this was going on, I would sometimes
stop and think to myself—and I mean really try to
grasp on a deep cognitive level, at least as deep as
you have to go to play jazz on a trombone—that here
I am, doing music in the most uncanny state knowable:

namely, as a living, breathing, conscious human
being—a claim some may find exaggerated, but,

nonetheless, one that would render me giddy with awe, and then utterly silent, because…well… consciousness? What's that anyway?

My guess is it's the very next question you come to after worrying yourself sick over: *Existence? How'd that happen? Who says it's gonna end someday? How? When? Where? Why?*

All I know we know for sure about consciousness is that we have it, and need it, to play jazz, and get gigs, and stay alive—which is an important part of *being* alive.

After which the vast majority of us die and fall unconscious. Or else we fall unconscious and die. Either way, by all outward appearances, our own little autographed copy of consciousness quietly fades away, leaving everyone else shaking their heads and saying (or at least thinking): *WTF?*

On top of all that, nobody knows exactly how we come into existence as conscious beings in the first place.

Sure, we know how we're made—the whole sexual procreation deal: *Stick this into that and rub till done.* But the greatest scientific minds out there can only agree about what the attributes of consciousness are; no one can explain how it happens or what it is specifically, except that the brain is somehow involved.

And not just *any* brain. Consciousness ain't no floozy.

One theory is that due to a particular organization of atoms, which all things are made of, consciousness emerged at some point in the development of higher organisms, producing a cool feeling of identity within the organism, and in some cases an even cooler feeling of selfhood—as in, *Hey what about me?*— accompanied quite often by that less cool feeling I mentioned: *WTF?*

Some say that consciousness is like a mirror, and
our thoughts and feelings like objects placed before
it. (And don't even ask where thoughts and feelings
come from. We'd need another whole poethon
to figure that one out.)

The mirror merely reflects images of the objects
(thoughts and feelings), without being changed by
them, and without judging them, or taking anything
personally, or getting stuck in all the emotional
gooeyness they usually come with. Like the ultimate
Teflon-coated impartial observer: *Aware—but
unaffected.*

If all that's true, the joke's on us, apparently, when
we feel bad about the bad stuff and good about the
good stuff—because our consciousness doesn't
feel a thing!

I suppose we could identify with consciousness,
then, instead of our thoughts and feelings, to chill
out and stay relaxed, like in mindfulness meditation.
But who's conscious enough to do that all day long?

As far as whether something is conscious or not,
there is a scientific theory going around that says a
thing is conscious *if it feels what it feels like to be
whatever it is.* (Finally—a scientific theory with no
scientific words in it that give you a headache.)

By this definition, human beings and mammals and
other animals are conscious. And, to a lesser or
greater degree, fish, insects, possibly even plants.

Whereas things like vinyl siding and a salami
sandwich likely aren't. And so you have to wonder
how some of us turn out to be humans, some of
us animals, some of us plants, and others the
sentient equivalent of a grinder.

Now that I'm alive and conscious, it feels like
I've won some kind of unexplainable, unattainable
prize. But how did I win it? Talent? Looks? Smarts?
Connections? Pity? A raffle? A terrible mistake?

Because here I am, experiencing life as a conscious
being, which my salami sandwich is not. My sandwich
did not win the same prize I did. Yet here it sits—with
mustard, tomato, and a nice thick slice of cheese—
which you have to assume is not conscious also.

And which brings us back to the main question:
Existence…how did it get here? And after it did,
how did *we* get here: You, me, my lunch, jazz?
And not only that, but where exactly is *here*?

These are the questions you'll need consciousness
for. Lots of it. Even just to think them up. Imagine
how much you'll need to answer them? Whoa!

When I think about what it means to be alive and
human and conscious, it blows my mind to realize
what an incredible stroke of luck it is that it happens
at all—to anyone—but mostly that it happened to me.

And then to think: Or I could have been an anteater,
or a eucalyptus tree, or vinyl siding, or a ham
sandwich… Sorry, but it bears repeating: *W-T-F?*

In the end, LIFE is the greatest prize. Without it,
you can forget about consciousness. Jazz, too.
We *the living* are the big winners. Granted, with a
fair amount of losers thrown in, for contrast's sake,
I suppose. Because it takes all kinds. Evidently.

And you know, as fascinating as all this is, it makes
me realize what a lousy jazz player I'd have been
if I sat around thinking about it all day. Which is
no way to stay alive as a sentient life form.

After a while, you just have to say, *Oh well, WTF?…*
and go back to working on your music. Otherwise,
I know one thing: I sure wouldn't want to hear me
play.

Looks to me like we may have a winner! One that's
kept me employed and eating since I got here.

And yet, you have to admit that consciousness is
the most profound acquired taste they've ever
found. In all of existence. For sure in this book.

We'd better check in with our distinguished panel of
experts, chosen from an earlier stanza to judge this
poetorial. Namely: the anteater, the eucalyptus tree,
the vinyl siding, and my personal favorite—the ham
sandwich—with mustard, tomato, and cheese, on a
bulky roll, sesame seed bagel, or gluten free wrap.

The judges are mulling it over. Nodding thoughtfully.
Looks like they've reached a consensus. I see four
satisfied smiles. The anteater is rising to speak directly
to the readers on the panel's behalf. Let's listen in…

Hey, how's everyone doing today? Y'all having fun?
What a great reading experience y'all have had, right?
Let's hear it for the author, Hal Crook. This guy can
really write, right? Heard he played jazz back in the
day. Trombone was it? Yikes. And he admits that?
Heard he was dropped as an infant once or twice.
That could explain it.

But what an imagination! Ending the book with a
talking anteater. So innovative…if a bit sophomoric.
Bet you won't find that in Keats or Eliot or Dickinson.
Early Whitman, maybe. Old Walt and I hung out.
He'd pace around the yard and talk his poet jive.
Whisper to the leaves. The grass. Himself. Me.

Anyway, it's an honor for us to be here. Especially
the vinyl siding, which never gets to go anywhere.
Once installed. Give a wave to the crowd, Vin.

Nice to see the kids up in the eucalyptus tree.
Watch out for splinters, you guys. And pythons.
And don't get hooked on that menthol. Trust me,
it's bad stuff. More addictive than termite larvae.
Tastier, too.

A reminder that the concession stand will be closing
in 30 minutes, so last call for a nice ham sandwich.

With all the fixins. Except hold the ham on mine,
being I'm just one big imaginary insectivore.

By the way, don't you love that shot of me on
the cover? Classic, right? Caught my good side.
I'll be signing copies in the parking lot. Stop by.
Bring the family. I'm here till midnight.

And now for the moment you've all been waiting for.
Heard you folks love a surprise ending. Heard you're
pretty good guessers, too. Want to give it a shot, then?

OK then, go for it…

Yup, you guessed it! On the very first try!
Jazz wins the poetorial! And the whole poethon!
Who would've thought, right? Talk about a surprise!
Hoo-ray for the HOME TEAM! Go-o-o-o Jazz!

Well, that's all the time we have today for the thrill
of victory and the agony of defeat. So, as soon as
y'all get your kids out of the jaws of that python,
kindly pick up your trash—including your food
wrappers and drink containers—and take it all
with you on your way out of the book.
Let's leave it in better condition than we
found it, OK? Shouldn't be too hard to do.

Meanwhile, happy trails. Be safe out there. Try not
to drop your infants. Check 'em for splinters, too.
And menthol addiction. And be sure to write a nice
review on Amazon. Remember: Every star helps.

HOME TEAM: Jazz 14; VISITORS: Acquired Tastes 13.

♫ ♫ ♫

Drawing by Zoe Crook, 1995, age 5.

HAL CROOK, Professor Emeritus, Berklee College of Music is an internationally known jazz musician, composer, arranger, and teacher. He has published four books on jazz improvisation, available at schott-music.com; one novel, *A Brief Madness: New Identity*; one collection of short stories, *Windborne Tales: Seven Stories*; and one collection of poetry, *Group Poems—Poetic Pieces: Flawed, Battered, and Fried*—available on Amazon.com and through booksellers everywhere.

Hal lives in Rhode Island with his wife, Joyce, and their feral cat, Sharon. *ADVENTURES IN POETRY: Poetorials on JAZZ and Other Acquired Tastes* is his second book of poetry.

www.halcrook.com

Your reaction to this book is important.
Please offer your thoughts and post a review on Amazon.

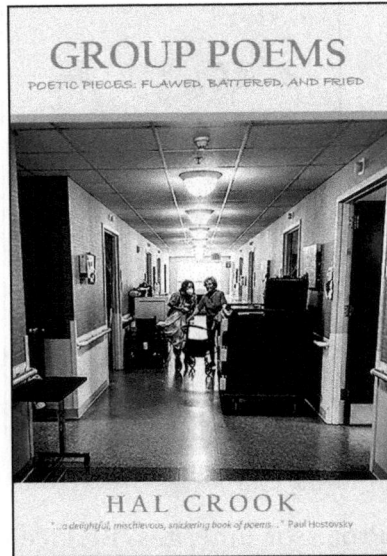

GROUP POEMS
POETIC PIECES: FLAWED, BATTERED, AND FRIED

HAL CROOK

"...a delightful, mischievous, snickering book of poems..." Paul Hostovsky

Praise for *GROUP POEMS*
Poetic Pieces: Flawed, Battered, and Fried

"Hal Crook steals poetry from the poets and gives it to the people, to whom it has always belonged anyway. He's a versifying Robin Hood, giving it back, paying it forward, pushing the proverbial envelope, pulling out all the metaphorical stops. He gives the *vulgus* what they want in a poem: a little vulgarity, a little kung fu, the wisdom of the sensei, the chutzpah of the putz, with a trombone chorus and some really sexy dancers in his head–it's all in his head–into which we are given a rare and lucky window with this delightful, mischievous, snickering, jazzy book of poems. *GROUP POEMS—Poetic Pieces: Flawed, Battered, and Fried* is a book to not only write home about but to carry home in your bare hands, and serve up its raw deliciousness to all your poetry-starved friends and loved ones."
Paul Hostovsky, author of *Mostly* and *Pitching for the Apostates*

"A natural writer with a rich vocabulary and a wicked wit, Hal Crook adds a new and distinctive voice to the world of poetry. He has thrown himself with vigor and enthusiasm into learning the ins and outs of making poems. And it shows. I watched the poems get better and better as the book took shape, every aspect of which is deliberate and well thought-out. I can't wait to read his next one." **Margie Keil Flanders, Managing Editor, *Crosswinds Poetry Journal*, author of *The Persuasive Beauty of Imperfection***

"This is a work of celebration and fun. It's poetry dancing in the streets rather than behaving for English class. It's poetry that doesn't wear a tie and that might have a patch or two sewn onto its trousers. I doubt that T. S. Eliot or Elizabeth Bishop would approve of these poems, but the folks who washed their socks or delivered their mail probably would..."
Rod Kessler, Professor Emeritus, Salem State University, author of *Off in Zimbabwe*

"Thoughtful, funny, delightfully irreverent. Hal Crook offers us a peak at life through his unique lens. With a successful "pre-poetry" career as a world-class jazz trombonist and educator, his wonderful sense of humor and perspective is peppered throughout. He was always a poet, anyway, through his music. Now, this! Highly recommended read."
Ken Amylon, Amica Insurance Executive

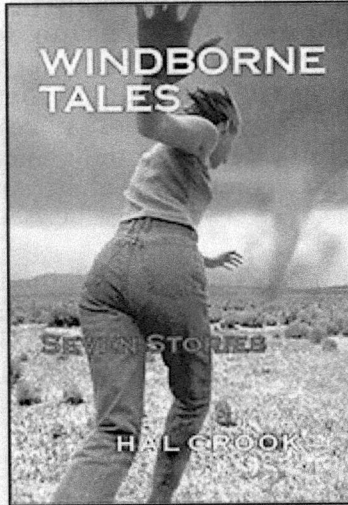

Praise for *WINDBORNE TALES: SEVEN STORIES*

"Great story telling. Fun, unpredictable, beautifully crafted, and always going somewhere, but…where? It's like one of Hal's jazz solos. You're not gonna know what it all means until the end of the last chorus. I felt I was in the hands of a trustworthy guide. All I had to do was sit back, turn pages, and enjoy the ride. Truly fantastic! And how many great trombone players would dare dream of playing the *Concerto for Trombone and Pen*. Only you Hal, only you."
Alan Silvestri, Film Composer: *Back to the Future Trilogy, Forrest Gump, Pinocchio, Who Framed Roger Rabbit, Predator, Romancing the Stone,* and 120 more.

"This collection of stories is as easy to read as it is hard to put down. Each tale is highly creative, thought-provoking, entertaining, and unique. The writing style is acerbic and wry. Characters are depicted in gritty detail, representing the worst—and at times the best—of humanity. On display is raw reality, unexpected twists and turns, and believable endings impossible to foretell. In 'Incident at Ponderosa East', the depravities and curiosities of the characters are vividly brought to life, as are their hopes and dreams. Clever and eloquently worded. Brilliant storytelling."
John Ferrara, Pianist/Author/Educator

"After a sterling debut novel—*A Brief Madness: New Identity*—Hal Crook has created this impressive collection of psychological gems. Part Bradbury, part Coben, part hipster, his combination of wit,

quasi-memoir and off-beat imagination captured my attention at every turn, and held it. In 'Covid Serenade' especially, the author encapsulates his unique existential vision of the human condition."
Paul Hoffman, LICSW/Therapist

"Hal Crook's stories get the pages turning by themselves. The characters are haunting creations. By the end of each tale, you feel you've gained a friend—and maybe an enemy! In any case, you're no longer alone. The writing stirs emotions you didn't know you had. In the story 'Windborne Tales', I found myself wondering: What if this happened to me?"
Nancy McDaniel, Artist/Accountant

"Each one of these unforgettable tales conveys what it means to be human. In 'All That Comes Our Way', the author brought me back to my childhood, vividly capturing not only how difficult it is to grow up, but how precious that experience is. And while reading 'Adventures in Jazz', I felt like I was part of the band, hanging out with Blue and his bandmates as they dealt with the stress of the tour and the challenges of living on the road. Constantly facing choices that pit the individuals' artistic goals against the success of the group."
Mark Esposito, Insurance Executive

"I reveled in this collection of tales, in which the novelist/jazz musician Hal Crook delves deftly into a broad spectrum of themes, gifting the reader with not just seven stories, but seven experiences—each one revealing a bit of the author's unique take on human nature, humor and humanity. And you'll never guess who the small brains are in 'Big Brains in Our Midst!'"
Jason Camelio, Trombonist/Guitarist, Global Education Professional

"*Windborne Tales: Seven Stories* is a must-read collection by novelist Hal Crook. These tales are full of likable and loathsome characters, and packed with delicious jazz references and a native son's take on Rhode Island. In 'Out With a Bang', readers experience the vagaries of life, love, loss and revenge, as though living through them ourselves. Top shelf, well crafted writing." **Greg Wardson, Pianist/ Educator**

"The stories in *Windborne Tales: Seven Stories* are timely, relevant, beautifully crafted and highly entertaining."
Curt Berg, Trombonist/Copyist

"No sophomore slump for this author! The stories in this collection are terrific. And unique. Spooky, funny, disturbing, entertaining. Think O. Henry writing for The Twilight Zone. They kept me up late—and not just while I was reading them." **Rick Bellaire, Founder, RI Music Hall of Fame**

"This book is music to my ears. Each story is unique and insightful, perfect in length, and exhibits great descriptiveness. Bravo Hal." **Gary B, Pianist/Computer Programmer**

"You can feel the world leaping from the author's mind to yours. The writing is creative, the characters grab your attention from the moment you meet them. Hal's humor the cherry on top." **Peter da Silva, Saxophonist/Educator**

"Hal Crook's unique voice carries through his stories, invoking a range of emotional modalities, taking readers on an unpredictable journey and liberating us from our habitual way of seeing the world." **DMM, Amazon Customer**

"*Windborne Tales: Seven Stories* is simply the best fiction I have read in many years, right up there with T. E. Lawrence's *The Seven Pillars of Wisdom*." **Miriam Rhodes, Amazon Customer**

"A master improviser turned writer—what's not to love? Seven stories that will stay with you, creating unforgettable characters and memorable images of Rhode Island, reminiscent of Stephen King's writing of Maine. Thoughtful, artful, thrilling, at times hilarious and at times heart wrenching. Just like life." **Daniel Rotem, Saxophonist/Educator**

"An excellent collection of fiction from a world class jazz trombonist and educator, proving that Hal is as adept at spinning a yarn as he is at improvising a chorus. He riffs, interweaves themes and motifs, and surprises the reader with unexpected turns, and does so with a sly sense of humor. Set in Rhode Island, the stories are unique and imaginative, with a through line that connects them. Musical references abound. A rewarding read." **Jim Peltz, Guitarist/Vocalist**

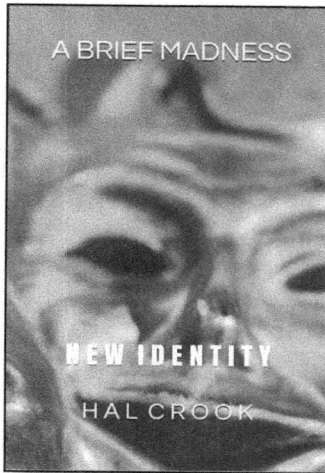

Praise for *A BRIEF MADNESS: NEW IDENTITY*

"This novel has a lot going for it. Both action and character nuance. The reader wants to know what will happen next, and what will happen to the characters. Agnes is a flawed, multidimensional heroine, whose actions give a moral ambiguity that deepens the novel's message. The jazz references and South Providence as a setting are rich and inviting. Some of Fleck's repartee with other characters is priceless." **Betty J. Cotter, Novelist/Writing Instructor**

"Great characters and story. Female African-American hero is smart and strong. Feels a bit like Walter Mosely. Quality writing with humor and grit." **Robert Nieske, Bassist/Educator**

"A suspenseful story, with interesting characters and at times hilarious dialogue." **Tom Gonnella, Attorney/Guitarist**

"The author expertly weaves history, intrigue, politics and humor throughout. Impossible to put down." **Julian Shore, Pianist/Educator**

"Unpredictable. Unique. Daring. Authentic. And entertaining." **Phil Mazza, Guitarist/Educator**

"It's a whopper of a thriller. I couldn't put it down. And at 95 years of age, I can't wait too much longer for a sequel!" **Peggy Smith, Bookkeeper**

"Terrific debut novel. Certainly in the upper echelon of crime fiction I've read in recent years." **Paul Hoffman, LICSW/Therapist**

"Characters are multidimensional and well developed…dark and disturbing antagonist, strong and persistent protagonist…balanced with humor and setting." **Mark Esposito, Insurance Executive**

"Expertly crafted first novel…a brutal and unforgiving trip through the changing nature of crime and punishment. A masterful achievement." **MJS, Amazon Customer**

"A thoughtful, engaging and convincing work of fiction…a genuine page turner." **John Ferrara, Pianist/Author/Educator**

"Fasten your seat belt and get ready for a thrill ride!" **Gene Roma, Percussionist/Educator**

"Perfect mixture of humor, compassion, suspense and terror. Kept me turning pages till 3 a.m." **Nancy McDaniel, Artist/Accountant**

"Exciting, well-written novel. Great characters and a roller coaster plot. A wild ride from beginning to end." **Greg Wardson, Pianist/Educator**

"Multidimensional villain and thought-provoking philosophical musings. Well-done first novel." **James Irelan, Guitarist/Poet**

"Superb, intelligent fiction…with action, humor, philosophy and great plot and character development. A cutting edge adventurous approach to prose." **Curt Berg, Trombonist/Copyist**

www.ingramcontent.com/pod-product-compliance
Lightning Source LLC
Chambersburg PA
CBHW060930040426
42445CB00011B/872